# THE REDEEMING POWER OF PRESENCE

### Andrew Carey

authorHOUSE®

*AuthorHouse™*
*1663 Liberty Drive*
*Bloomington, IN 47403*
*www.authorhouse.com*
*Phone: 1-800-839-8640*

*First published by AuthorHouse      10/1/2010*

*ISBN: 978-1-4520-5184-0 (sc)*
*ISBN: 978-1-4520-5185-7 (hc)*
*ISBN: 978-1-4520-5186-4 (e)*

*Library of Congress Control Number: 2010913200*

*Printed in the United States of America*

*This book is printed on acid-free paper.*

*Note: The New International Version and the New American Standard are the biblical translations used throughout. Occasionally, certain scriptures are italicized for added emphasis.*

## ACKNOWLEDGEMENTS

First and foremost, I want to thank the Lord for His unfailing love and faithfulness that patiently and endlessly work to free me, just as He does for each of us – to free our true selves so as to know and express His love on this earth. Second, I thank my wife Kathy for her faithfulness to the Lord and to our marriage and family. I am thankful for her gifts of thoughtfulness, relational ways, and expressiveness that continue to challenge and teach me about what nurturance, relationship, and childlikeness are. Also, I want to thank my sons, as well as my parents, for their encouragement and part they played in me being shaped a little more into the person I am today.

In addition, I want to thank those I fellowship with, especially Joel, Michelle, Mike, Laurie, John, and Ben for the ways that their love, acceptance, wisdom, and honesty have supported, challenged, and freed me to grow in the Lord. Thanks as well to my students and colleagues who have encouraged, supported, and challenged me to stretch further in my understanding of the human experience. Also, I want to thank all the forerunners who have participated with the Lord in the way of the cross and in the way of being present and awakened in life. We are all one body who play a part in our collective journey of being present and awakened in true relationship with the Lord.

As far as support for rereading drafts of this book, I especially want to thank Mary Grist and Laurie Carey. Their input and suggestions very much helped to clarify and refine the final messages that you see.

Likewise, the publishing team at Authorhouse, Team Pearl, was very dedicated and skilled in bringing about a quality book. The cover designs are fabulous, and the interior design, as well, was exactly what I was looking for. I want specifically to thank Amanda, Margaret, Erin, Patty, Betsy, and Dan for their contributions that will hopefully make a difference in people's lives through "The Redeeming Power of Presence."

# CONTENTS

# INTRODUCTION

Have you felt like a part of you knows that life is meant to be something more than it currently is? Have you looked around and seen all the suffering and pain, possibly within yourself as well, and thought that life is ultimately to be more than we know as life? Have you sometimes experienced Christianity as a lot of words and yet wondered "Where is the powerful presence of the Lord, a living presence that is beyond mere words?" I have asked these kinds of questions along my journey as well, especially during times of struggle. Even present day Christianity as a whole was not what I believed the Lord was ultimately after.

To me, there seemed to be some larger purpose and way that we had not yet truly walked into as Christians, a way that looks much more like Jesus walked while on this earth. This way that seemed to open up very quickly to me is a way that powerfully brings redemption and restoration. Deeper healing and transformation into greater likeness of the Lord are truly possible, a transformation that reaches out with and expresses His love that draws all unto Himself.

This powerful pathway that opened up to me, really, that found me, is walking regularly in the present moment with the presence of the Lord. This pathway is more than "practicing the Lord's presence" that I had learned in earlier years, which was focused on watching for the Lord and what He does in life. That learning was about paying attention to the Lord's presence but still overlooked the fact that I might not be truly present with Him so as to receive His presence and, therefore, His grace. That original learning had been very helpful, and yet, I have now experienced a pathway that has produced much greater restoration and freedom than that previous learning, and even more than I thought was possible. I have found that knowing and expressing the Lord's love as well as His other fruits is only readily accessible when I remain in the present moment where He and His grace abide.

While walking in the present with the Lord's presence might sound simple in some ways, as you read you will discover that the majority of people rarely remain in the present moment because, like pin balls bouncing around, their minds regularly and seemingly uncontrollably take them into the past or the future; and even when they think they are present focused, they often look at it through a lens from their past. Because the Lord allows free will, we constantly come out of relationship with Him when we leave the present moment in our minds. To be in relationship with the Lord requires remaining in the present moment where His presence reigns as "I Am." That is where His grace and love abide. That is where He is truly *living* water that satisfies beyond mere words.

True redemption and restoration are found in the presence of the Lord. Healing, physically and spiritually, happens through us being joined with the presence of the Lord such that the power of His presence, love, and light can touch and redeem us in the places of darkness and disease. When Jesus healed people, it was through His presence, not through mere words; and it was a presence that was larger than earthly life – a presence that we as yet truly know little about because of not being in the present much with Him.

Jesus' healing powers resulted from being present with the Father's presence, and that Presence brought love, light, and redemption into lost places. For us, new light is brought to us through being joined with Christ's presence in places that lack the Lord and His Love. As a whole, we have not yet really learned the

Way of aligning ourselves with the Lord Who is in us and greater than us such that His light and watchful eye from within begin to expose and transform all that is not light. As we learn to walk further in this way of being in the present moment with Him, however, the light of His presence begins to fill our whole body with light – and all must bow to the Lord.

Walking regularly in the present moment with Christ is a powerful way of walking that releases God's rights and love in and through us on this earth. And yet, for my own journey, I have much to learn about walking this way that Jesus walked. I am not one who has arrived at some glorious place of ongoing presence and unwavering faith. Where Jesus said the ruler of this world had "nothing in Him," I am one who has struggled like others to truly leave the attachments of this world such that it would have little hold over me. Still, I have experienced great joy and freedom regarding what the Lord has done in a tremendously short time in my walk of learning to be present in each moment. Learning to be present with the Lord has been a tremendous gift to me and to the others I fellowship with. We are extremely grateful for this gift and believe that the Lord desires, as well, to give this gift to others who have ears to hear.

Becoming more present has been a significant factor in the Lord more powerfully moving me out of the bondage of the old self and into a more victorious place of walking in ongoing awareness of the Lord's presence and goodness. While this kind of walk is always a process, walking in the present moment with Christ has allowed me to have true "choices" available that definitely had not been available previously. I didn't realize that I had a greater degree of "choice" available to me than I knew regarding not succumbing to unwanted thoughts or emotions controlling me in certain areas. While I outwardly followed Christ fairly well, inwardly I had still been concerned about what others thought of me and I would bow to fear in various difficult people situations. I shut down inwardly while still going through the motions outwardly of doing what I believed the Lord wanted of me. Love was neither experienced by me nor free to truly reach and touch others through me when inwardly I was filled with fear in those ways.

Since learning to be present with the Lord in a more ongoing way, however, those unwanted thoughts and emotions have greatly dissipated. While I still have moments of those distractions at various points, being more regularly present each moment has filled me with the Lord's thoughts and fruits, enabling me to love beyond the restricted ways I had walked previously. *To the extent that I remain present, that is to the extent that I am able to "remain awake" and to know the Lord's presence along with the fruits of the Spirit.* In areas that I had no real hope of change, I found the Lord miraculously changing me.

To me personally, learning to be present with Christ as a way of walking in life feels like a great secret or mystery that part of me wishes I had known long ago – and yet, I know that Christ's time is right and that "now" was the right time and is always the right time. In addition, my sense is that this journey of learning to walk regularly in the present moment with the Lord is a "narrow way" that is truly a significant pathway for learning some of the greater mysteries of Christ that are still to come.

The mysteries of Christ are great, and learning to be present with Him is one of those mysteries. Christ continues to release more of these mysteries as we head into the latter days. No single voice or gift is the answer. While the Lord is one Lord, His body has many parts. To embrace the fullness of Christ and His gifts to us, we must embrace the various voices and parts of Him that are used for communicating the whole. While we are to discern according to the scriptures His voices that He uses for making us more whole, holy, or complete in Him, we are to continue opening up to fuller revelations of Him. I say this because this book will likely challenge and stretch you beyond the boundaries of what is familiar and comfortable to you – but, it will likely bring many fresh revelations and cause much growth in the Lord as well, whether or not you end up agreeing with some of what has been expressed in these writings. Wrestling through what it is that you truly believe always produces growth.

The reason the latter times will be greater than the former is because the Lord will come in greater fullness in His people than ever before. Greater fullness means greater revelations of Him – which can only occur through opening up to more of Him than we have known of Him previously. Growing into Him is a life-long journey, and anytime we put Him into finite boxes of who we determine Him to be, we disallow fuller revelations of Him. Christ is relational, complete, and the full expression of love. As we continue to hear His voice more fully, we will sense and be drawn more into connectedness, completeness, and love. In contrast, when we hear a voice that is not of Christ, we often experience and are drawn into greater judgment, separateness, and incompleteness. Pay attention to the various voices of Christ that gather people unto Him, for all things will be gathered into Christ in the end.

Along with the scriptures, Christ in you (Col. 1:27), the hope of glory, is your true Guide that leads you in His Way. When the voice of truth speaks, whoever it may happen to speak through at a given point, you will sense your heart resonating with that Truth – for it is He that causes your heart to resonate in that way when He speaks. Just as it states in the scriptures (see 1 Jn. 2:27), "You have no need of a teacher," for your Guide, or Teacher, is within you. While there are many voices, there is one true Teacher or Guide. Let your Guide lead and teach you as you read further, for this book is one voice of the many parts of His voice. Becoming present with Christ is one gift of the many gifts for bringing healing and meeting the various needs that He desires to meet. For the more you become healed and whole through becoming present with Him, the more He and His love will be freed to love through you. You will know this truth the more you become present, because the more you become present, the more you become freed, and the more you become freed in Him, the more His love will compel you to leave all and love.

Note: As you read further, you may want to take your time and read aloud because reading aloud tends to engage more of your senses and more of who you truly are, which sometimes deepens your experience and opens more of a way for the Spirit. Slowing down, as well, allows you to be more present and to take in what you read. Also, you will find that this book is not so much a "how-to" book as it is a book simply to read and let the power of the Lord work what He wishes to work into your life in His time – for *striving to attain presence will undermine the very presence and relationship with the Lord you desire.* So feel free simply to read and let the Lord do all the work, and to reread the book, if you wish, at a later point for deepening the Lord's work. Following each chapter, as is the case here as well, are two or three statements in which to be still and present with so as to allow the Lord some time to work His works deeper within you. And if the Lord so chooses, at a certain point, to move you to action regarding applying to your life what you have read, then yield to Him in action as well.

*Be still, and be; become aware of your present experience and how the Lord may be stirring your heart at the moment. Know that He is the LIVING God and is truly within you.*

# Presence: The Foundation of All Good Things

A great teacher of the scriptures, T. Austin-Sparks, once said that when learning about a particular topic in the scriptures, it is important to see God's first as well as last and final word about the topic. Regarding the presence of the Lord, I would like us to pay attention to God's final word on the subject and then go back and see the contrast of the first place that that topic comes onto the scene.

"And I saw a great white throne and Him who sat upon it, *from whose presence* earth and heaven fled away, and no place was found for them" (Rev. 20:11). What is the awesome power that causes even heaven and earth as we have known them to flee away in the end? The Lord's presence. Whatever is not of God simply will not stand in the presence of the Lord in the end. Only that which is built upon His foundation will stand, for He is the foundation of all lasting things. Only that which is of Him will remain. That is why we will be changed into His likeness. His presence, which is light, will cause all things to become light in the end – and that which is not, will fall away. But what is the power that causes all of this? It is simply the presence of the Lord. In similar fashion to what the presence of the Lord does, the scriptures state (2 Ptr. 3:10-13), "But the day of the Lord will come like a thief, in which the heavens will pass away with a roar and the elements will be destroyed with intense heat, and the earth and its works will be burned up. Since all these things are to be destroyed in this way, what sort of people ought you to be in holy conduct and godliness, looking for and hastening the coming of the day of God, on account of which the heavens will be destroyed by burning, and the elements will melt with intense heat! But according to His promise we are looking for new heavens and a new earth, in which righteousness dwells."

We are looking for new heavens and a new earth in which righteousness (or God's rights) dwells. Can you hear in the above verses how God's presence alone causes all to fall away that is not of Him and, as well, brings forth His rights? In other words, *through God's presence, all His rights and therefore all His fruits are birthed.* I used to think that love was the most important attribute of God's for me to pay attention to in my walk. While I still think that love describes the greatest essence and gift of who God is to us, I now see His presence as more valuable to become awakened to in our daily walk. Love cannot exist without God's presence – and love cannot regularly exist in the reality of our lives on this earth without us being present to be one-with His presence. This means that without the Lord's presence, we cannot truly know love or express love. Love depends on God's presence, and us being present with His presence is foundational for regularly experiencing and expressing the reality of His love. Being present so as to experience God's presence is the foundation for all good things.

While the presence of the Lord melts away all that is not Him and transforms into light all that is exposed by light (Eph. 5:13), we now likely have an obvious question to answer regarding the practicality of our walk. If the presence of the Lord is that powerful to further transform us into His likeness, why has this not already fully occurred? Why do we not walk in a much greater place of redemption, healing, and love like Jesus walked? **We as a whole do not begin to understand the extent that we are not**

**present and available to the Lord and His presence. We greatly underestimate the extent that we constantly hide from and even disallow the presence of the Lord**.

When humanity sinned and fell from grace, we have continued, often unknowingly, repeating much of what Adam and Eve initially did in the garden (Gen. 3:8): "And they heard the sound of the Lord God walking in the garden in the cool of the day, and the man and his wife *hid themselves from the presence* of the Lord God among the trees of the garden." They hid themselves from the presence of the Lord. When they hid themselves from God's presence, they did so not just physically, but mentally and psychologically. That was the blindness. While the Lord and His presence were evident in the garden, Adam and Eve did not and could not know the Lord's love or His other fruits because they entered a state of hiding themselves from His presence. So, in actuality, the fall from grace was also a "fall" or retreat from God's presence.

Presence goes hand in hand with grace. Do you hear that although God's presence causes all things to bow in the end, we can mentally and psychologically hide ourselves from the presence of the Lord and therefore not receive of His grace or love? In a sense, because of our free will we can disallow true contact with the Lord's presence. The fall was a fall from presence – from the Presence that provides grace. From the point of the fall, Adam and Eve were deceived not to know how much they hid themselves from God's presence; and today, we are still greatly deceived regarding how much we continually hide from the Lord's presence even when we outwardly very much want His presence. It has been the natural way of humanity since the fall.

*Be still; let the Lord stir your heart about the power of His presence that is able to perform all the necessary work of transforming us and drawing us to Him – as we simply learn to be present with Him.*

# Presence: Hide and Seek

In response to our hiding, the Lord *seeks* to find and be with that which is lost (Lk. 19:10). Seek is a strong word and rarely used regarding the Lord. But here it is, revealing His fervency to pursue us with His love. He fervently desires fellowship and being with us in the lost places. He came not to be with the healthy, but with the sick (because He already is with the truly healthy). Jesus emphasized (Lk. 15:7), "I tell you that in the same way, there will be more joy in heaven over one sinner who repents, than over ninety-nine righteous persons who need no repentance." The Lord is active and fervent in His pursuit of being with us in the lost places -- in unbelievers as a whole, and within believers in the places that are still lost.

While it is true that the Lord fervently seeks to be with us in the places that are lost, and that His presence alone simply transforms us, we must be in union with the presence of the Lord in those places for transformation to occur. Overall, God does not do these works *to* us. The Lord created us for relationship with Him and, as a whole, He will not violate free will and force Himself upon us. If God regularly violated free will to be with us, it would not be "relationship" or fellowship with us. Our being with Him would not be from free will. The Lord desires that we would freely want and learn to be in relational union with Him. It is union with the presence of the Lord that mightily transforms us into His likeness. Even Jesus became perfect (meaning complete) through remaining present with the Father's presence through all His sufferings.

The Lord's presence is always with us, and yet, we through our own idols and ways are often not in union with His presence; and in a sense, He does not know us there (or us Him) as seen in the scriptures (Lk. 13:25-27), "Once the head of the house gets up and shuts the door, and you begin to stand outside and knock on the door, saying, 'Lord, open up to us!' then He will answer and say to you, 'I do not know where you are from.' Then you will begin to say, 'We ate and drank in Your presence, and You taught in our streets'; and He will say, 'I tell you, *I do not know where you are from*; depart from Me, all you evildoers'." Do you see? We might have been aware of the Lord or even have done lots of things that we thought were for Him but were never really in relationship or union with Him during all those things. He wants to know us relationally, not be aware of us or simply "use" us. Only through us knowing Him and His love and being in union with Him are we able to experience, and be a vessel for, His true fruits coming through us. Relationship and knowing the Lord bring true fruits, not our doings. Without relationship with Him, the works are really all our own works that are at least partly selfishly motivated in the end, and He will say "Depart from me you evildoer."

When we are not in union with the Lord and His presence, we will not only remain unchanged, but we will not know relationship, love, and the fruits of His Spirit as a whole. Knowing the ongoing goodness of the Lord depends upon union with Him and His presence. We normally have no clue, however, about how much we are turned other directions in a way that we do not allow His presence to be with us. And probably the single most tragic way that we do not allow His presence to be in contact with us is in our lost or darker places. This is so because we have bought the many lies about Him who is holy not being able to be with us in our places of sin. And, actually, that is the root of the overall blindness that Adam and Eve were deceived by as well, which is what caused them to hide from the presence of the Lord after sinning. They could no longer see God and His love accurately.

After the fall, Adam and Eve didn't know they could be loved and touched by God even in their places of sin. While it is true that too much holiness and presence of God all at once could destroy people because of their sins, especially if they arrogantly or inappropriately forced themselves upon His presence, it is not because His holiness cannot touch sin. In fact, the Lord touching and being present with us, and with our sin and places of lostness, is *how* we become healed and restored. Our being present with His presence, especially in our lost places, is how sin and darkness are dissolved. But we so often disallow the Lord's presence in our darker places, especially because of believing that holiness cannot be with sin. And so we hide while the Lord continues to seek, and we wonder why we are not healed and changed more powerfully than we are. Our holding the Lord away or hiding from His presence is the topic desperately needing addressed before we continue with how to be in union with His presence and what His presence does.

*Be still; be present and know how much the Lord simply wants relationship with us – in all aspects of our lives.*

# HIDING FROM PRESENCE
# BECAUSE OF THE PERCEIVED CHASM

While the chasm that is shown on many Christian tracts has been used for great good, it has also been misleading and actually conveys an inaccurate message. For example, the chasm that is illustrated on the tracts is often taught about in a way that portrays God as so holy that He cannot be with us until we believe in and confess Him as Lord. That way of treating our "relationship" with the Lord puts a burden or responsibility on us first to be in relationship with Him. Something is required of us prior to being loved and accepted. Yet, it is always the Lord who initiates with us first (we love because He first loved us – 1 Jn. 4:19). The chasm portrayed in that manner also conveys the Maker as a somewhat harsh God with a disdain for the people He made until they do something He requires of them. It portrays God, the Maker, as one who is not at all able to be with what He made without something initiated from their end. Similarly, another unintended message is that sin is more powerful than God's holiness. For instance, God does not have to bow to or wait on sin to change before He can touch us. Rather, He and His holiness are greater than sin. He *can* touch sin. Christ died for us and came to be with us and open our eyes while we were still sinners (Rom. 5:8).

Jesus, God's picture of holiness, first touched the leper (a clear picture of uncleanness and unholiness) and then healed him (Mk. 1:41). I'm sure that those witnessing that experience gasped with horror – because all the teachings had indicated that one should never touch that which is unclean if they wanted to remain holy. They knew the parallel teaching from the Old Testament that rotten fruit always defiles the good fruit. That principle, earthly speaking, *is* always true. That is why Jesus blatantly touched the leper first. He boldly *wanted* to dispel that lie so that we would clearly know that He (and His love) is beyond the laws of this earth.

Love wants to, and is able to, be with sin. Jesus could have healed the leper without touching Him at all just as He had healed many others with a spoken word. Yet, Jesus deliberately touched the leper to show us that He who is truly holy can and desires to touch us in our places of sin and uncleanness. This spiritual law is evident in Jesus' actions, even before the event of the cross had occurred. That is also why Jesus washed the disciples' feet, and yet, similar to Peter (see Jn. 13:8), our first inclination is "You should not wash or touch me who is unclean!" The problem of us not being touched by the Lord in our places of lostness or uncleanness has never been on God's end. Rather, we have plainly disallowed Him to touch us and be with us in our places of sin and lostness. While God needs to touch us patiently and gradually in many ways in our lives so we don't become destroyed in the process, holiness can and does touch sin. That is His presence touching us in the sinful places, and that is how we are healed. That is how we are redeemed.

Do you recognize the misleading and daunting separateness from God that people would experience when seeing the chasm as portrayed on the tracts? There may be some who will still staunchly stand on the side of "But there is separateness because of sin." While we definitely do experience separateness in our places of sin, believer and nonbeliever alike, it is not from God's end. The cross, and the "dividing wall" have to do with the enmity on our end. Because of sin's deceptive lies, we do not know the truth of love and forgiveness first for sins right where we are. In Ephesians, it states (2:16-18), "… through the cross, by it having put to death the enmity. And He came and preached peace to you who were far away, and peace to those who were near; for through Him we both have our access in one Spirit to the Father." Any wall between us and God is because of our false conclusions about Him. We tend to see God the way the world has treated us. That is, we have to perform well and be mistake free, and then the world can love us. Typically, we have a very difficult time believing that God can and actually does love us first. In fact, we learn to love because He first loves us. Love is always available. That is why Jesus said that He never leaves or forsakes us. Since the time of Adam and Eve, however, we have continually bought the enemy's lie that God cannot really love us presently when we have sinned or performed inadequately – and we hide from God's presence. There is no true chasm from God's end.

We may ask, however, "But what about the need for the cross, the blood, and a sacrifice for sins that Christ's purpose was all about? Wasn't there a need for that?" While the law did state that nearly everything needed to be cleansed by blood (Heb. 9:22), the law and the earlier covenants were *not* the true or the real. They were only shadows, copies, and, in a sense, still not fully accurate because they were not complete (see 8:5-7). Those things only pointed in the direction of a reality that could not yet be received by man (and that we still have much difficulty receiving). The writer of Hebrews continues (10:1): "The law is only a shadow of the good things that are coming --- not the realities themselves." He then emphasizes that the blood of goats and bulls could never really take away sins, and that a sacrifice was not what God ever really desired – but a "body prepared for Him" by Christ doing His will (see verses 3-7). *God's people could automatically receive His presence and redemption if they would but be present and in relationship with Him rather than hiding.* Finding (and really God providing) a Vessel that would be in relationship with Him was what God was always after. A body prepared for Him.

With a Vessel in relationship with God, He and His rights could come through that Vessel and reach others. Relationship, and being present with His Presence, could now finally begin with God's people. It only takes one Vessel on earth who trusts God and His love, and thus, is truly in relationship with Him such that His rights could come pouring through to draw other vessels in this relational way. The cross, then, was centered on bringing God's rights to this earth through a Vessel, while still allowing true relationship and free will. For bringing about relationship, however, the work of Jesus' blood on the cross was most about "cleansing us from a guilty conscience." Do you hear? What is our guilty conscience centered on? When we have sinned or "done wrong," we simply don't know love and forgiveness very well at those places, and thus, we avoid relationship and being present – with God and others. That is the guilty conscience at work. Since the time of Adam and Eve, and still the most predominant struggle of the day, we do not believe and trust the love that God has for us when we have sinned or performed poorly. You can hear this difficult journey when John states (1 Jn. 4:19), "And we have *come to know and have believed the love* which God has for us." Their guilty consciences needed cleansed so as to trust God's love in places that made no earthly sense.

Along with a guilty conscience comes distrust of the Lord, and thus, self-preservation. When we don't know God and His love at our places of darkness and sin, there is no trust of Him. Self-preservation and "taking" become the norm because of underlying fear and shame about not being able to be loved. So we self-protect and we take because of not being able to trust God's love.

In the garden of Eden, Adam and Eve hid from God's presence because they couldn't trust God's love for them once they had sinned. They would not let His love touch and redeem them in that place of sin because of a guilty conscience. The cross was to show us what was always true – that God came to be present with and love sinners – such that His presence could touch us and restore us from sin. As a people we simply wouldn't ever believe it, and even after the cross, we still struggle to believe it. We still need much grace and help from the Lord to have our guilty consciences cleansed (guilty consciences because of not knowing love when we sin and perform poorly). If you want to see more of this area addressed scripturally, about our unbelief that causes us not to enter rest, and about our consciences needing cleansed, read the whole book of Hebrews. See especially Hebrews about the warnings regarding our lack of belief and inability to enter God's rest, which is really because of not knowing and trusting His love when we "fall short": 3:19; 4:1; and 4:10-11. For learning more about the central purpose of the cross for cleansing us from our guilty consciences (and subsequently sin), see Hebrews 9:8-9; 9:12-14; and 10:19-23.

What prepares the way for receiving love? Knowing the forgiveness of sins "prepares the way" and essentially "allows" one to truly know and receive the fullness of Love. That is why John the Baptist came first to prepare the way for Jesus. The whole connection between John the Baptist and Jesus was to dramatically portray that which prepares the way for receiving the fullness of Love. When Zechariah prophesied about his son, John the Baptist, he stated (Lk. 1:76-78), "And you, my child, will be called a prophet of the Most High; for you will go on before the Lord to prepare the way for Him, to give His people the knowledge of salvation *through the forgiveness of their sins*, because of the tender mercy of our God ...". We can hear through these verses that the people could know salvation and be prepared to receive Jesus *through* first knowing the forgiveness of sins. To say this in another way, people could not truly receive Jesus, or Love, and could not receive and experience His redeeming power without first knowing the forgiveness of sins. People needed to know that they could be loved where they were, with sins essentially overlooked or not held against them. Then they could receive and know Love and its redeeming power. Their guilty consciences would be cleansed such that they could know they were able to be loved in spite of their sins. That is what enabled the people to come to Jesus. That is also why John the Baptist cried out (Lk. 3:4), "Prepare the way of the Lord, make straight paths for Him." The way that straight paths are made for Him is to know the forgiveness of sins where we currently are first. Then we can truly receive Jesus.

In fact, not truly knowing the forgiveness of sins, of being accepted where we are in spite of sins, is likely the single most powerful obstacle in the way of coming to know the redeeming power of the Lord. While this is a significant obstacle initially needing broken in all people, some people will resist this learning more fully because of the power and impact of earlier life training about imperfection and sin. Until unacceptance of imperfection and sin is overcome, much of abiding in the present moment will seem unreachable – at least to regularly walk in the present moment. Because unacceptance of sin, self, or life in any way constantly takes us out of the reality of the present moment, those who struggle more significantly with the issue of unacceptance of imperfection and sin will likely need to pray and ask for the Lord first for grace regarding overcoming this issue. If acceptance of imperfection and sin within self is a significant struggle for you, the wisdom from my own journey would say to look to the Lord to work on this area for a while before moving on to trying to learn more about becoming regularly present. While you may choose to continue reading this book, just know that you will likely struggle in walking in the present moment until you first learn to accept yourself sin and all. If you are unaccepting of imperfection and sin within self, you will regularly come out of the present moment – because significant unacceptance of sin is essentially a powerful "body pain" from the past that works constantly to overtake and dominate you (discussed further in chapter 13).

Once we come to a certain point in our walk, to go further

with the Lord means having the unacceptance of our sins broken before all else. What I mean is this: you will have some area of sin that the Lord will not give the grace to change until you first accept yourself as you are, and, to know His acceptance there as well. He wants you to know love and have relationship with Him right where you are. In other words, the Lord doesn't want you going on without knowing Him accurately this way; He doesn't want you to think His love of you is based upon your earthly perfection. So the Lord will leave you "stuck" in a place of having to see your sin over and over until you become broken and humbled about the fact that you have absolutely no power to change sin. *That is when a shift of power can begin in your life.*

You may think that you already know that you cannot change. I would say that you are deceiving yourself, as long as you have any energy toward unacceptance of yourself as you are. That energy shows the unacceptance, and that part of you still thinks you should be able to change. For me, when I was being broken about this issue of unacceptance of self as I was, I paid attention for absolutely any energy that revealed even slight irritation toward myself upon becoming aware of imperfection or sin. When I saw irritation or even a clipped energy toward myself in some form, I knew that I had not yet accepted imperfection and sin. I knew that I did not yet know True Love where I was. I knew, as well, that I was not to look for any other lesson because I could tell that He only wanted me paying attention to this crucial lesson until it was learned.

When you become broken and humbled regarding your sin, your earthly energy stops connected to that sin and simply allows it to be. Your earthly power to try to change sin finally becomes broken and humbled. Gradually, upon acceptance of sin and self, you come to a place of rest and awareness of the Lord's goodness and love of you there. Once you have had a season of accepting yourself (rather than fighting life), the Lord begins to bring grace that somehow seems to bring change as well to the sinful area – and you knew that you had absolutely nothing to do with it. That is when, at an experiential level, you become aware of the Lord's power to save. You become aware of the greatness of the Lord's love and His personal care for you in your life. You also realize that, until that point, beneath your awareness you had worked at becoming good enough and doing works "for" Him. And now, by paying attention to the energy within self during places of evident sin in your life, you can see whether the unacceptance of imperfection and sin is alive and well or whether that taskmaster has been broken. Brokenness about not being able to change self and its sin is the key to breaking the power of the old self. And the power of the old self becoming broken and humbled is crucial for beginning to know the redeeming power of the Lord.

Even when John the Baptist cried out "repent," it was along the lines of "Allow change about the way you are walking regarding sin; you have believed that you must either change yourself or hide in shame connected to your sins, but I say allow the Lord's forgiveness to reach and wash over you so that you would know the fullness of His peace and love where you are as He touches you in those places of sin." *If we don't know the security of the forgiveness of sins first, of being loved where we are first, we will be fearful, unbelieving, and distrustful of God and Love.* The Pharisees are a great example or symbol of not having known the forgiveness of sin, and that lack of knowing forgiveness manifested in their adverse reactions toward Jesus. The Pharisees did not receive Jesus (Love) because they had not first received the baptism of John, which was the forgiveness of sins. The scriptures state (Lk. 7:29-30), "And when all the people and the tax-gatherers heard this, they acknowledged God's justice, having been baptized with the baptism of John. But the Pharisees and the lawyers rejected God's purpose for themselves, not having been baptized by John." Knowing the forgiveness of sins is crucial for trusting and truly receiving Jesus. Knowing forgiveness and acceptance is also key to not rejecting God's purposes for us.

When two people in conflict are individually at a place of

insecurity regardless of their differences, the root cause beneath awareness is typically that neither knows compassion and love at those places of difficulty and insecurity. When people sin, invariably at their core is not knowing or being grounded in forgiveness of sins, and therefore, not truly knowing love. Only through knowing forgiveness and love do we become freed from sin. Regardless of the issue or the differing places of sin within people (regarding conflict or otherwise), we are all exactly the same inside: the place of difficulty within is always rooted in not knowing the forgiveness of sins and, therefore, not truly knowing or trusting love or Jesus there.

As illustrated above, John's baptism of the forgiveness of sins opened the way and allowed people to make straight paths so as to receive Jesus. Since the final event of the cross, however, people can know symbolically through the cross that receiving Jesus means knowing up front that our sins are already forgiven. Nothing more is needed for forgiveness to occur because forgiveness is a given up front. It is through knowing that our sins are already forgiven that our guilty consciences are cleansed, and knowing this security of forgiveness and being loved first as we are, then, is how we can receive the fullness of Love (Christ). In fact, if you haven't truly known the security of being loved where you are in spite of certain sinfulness (or something wrongful within you that seems unable to be "fixed"), I would venture to say that you have not truly known Jesus and His love – at the very least, that would be the case in that area of lack within you.

In short, there is no true chasm between God and people (for believers or unbelievers) *except in our minds*, in that we typically "hide from the Lord's presence" in places that we don't know or believe Him and His love that are greater than any of our sins. We regularly hide from His presence that has the power to continually cleanse us from our sinful ways of walking in life. Believers still regularly have guilty consciences in their places of darkness and sin, and in shame they hide from the Lord's presence there. Unbelievers often don't know God and His love in an overall way, and therefore do not allow His presence in general. I realize that this way of viewing unbelievers is likely challenging and different than much of what has been taught previously. But the only "block" or "chasm" for unbelievers is that they do not allow God to love them in a more overall way – similar to how believers still do not allow God to love them in certain, lost aspects of their lives. When we disallow the Lord's love in those ways, we are much like the Pharisees that did not receive the truth about the forgiveness of sins and, therefore, are unable to receive Jesus in those sinful places. Like the Pharisees, we disallow His presence there.

Jesus didn't initially ask those He healed to confess Him first as Lord (there was no chasm). They were yet unable to make such a confession because of the "darkness" of a guilty conscience. Instead, Jesus loved, touched, and healed them first when they allowed Him and His presence to do so. Love plainly wanted to be with them and had always wanted to be with them, sin and all. It was Jesus' touch of the leper's sin and uncleanness that healed his guilty conscience. The leper would have known at once that Jesus could be with Him without some action or performance required on his end first. Just watching the way Jesus walked and how He was present with others, those around Him would have immediately known that He wanted to be with them in spite of their sin, with no requirement first. In other words, the people that got to experience Jesus' presence already knew that He forgave and overlooked their sins simply by how He interacted with them. Nothing was held against them, and nothing was expected of them. With Jesus' presence touching and being with people first, then they began to know Him as Lord. Then, they began to know and experience redemption, healing, and restoration from a guilty conscience.

Are you beginning to get a sense of how much, like Adam and Eve, we have bought lies that the Lord cannot or does not want to be with us until we make ourselves clean first? Be present and pay attention to the Lord's greater presence within you. As you pay attention to your inner sense that is joined with His presence, inwardly you already know the truth of the true nature of His unfailing love.

*Cease striving; stop trying to change yourself, and even stop reading if you have difficulty accepting imperfection and sin within you. Cease your earthly energy so that His energy can emerge and transform you. Know that He loves you first, right where you are now, with no striving needed to be at some further, better place – there is no chasm except the lies we believe.*

# CHRIST AND HIS PART: THE PRESENCE THAT DESIRES TO JOIN WITH THE LOW PLACES

Jesus came in humility as a baby. As a Man, He was put on the cross as a criminal and was despised; He died without any earthly riches. "He made Him who knew no sin to be sin on our behalf, that we might become the righteousness of God in Him" (2 Cor. 5:21). Can you hear? How low did God have to go to be with us? He went as low as possible, to the point that He became sin on our behalf. That is joining us as low as can be. Through this Way, Love, from a low position as a true and secure foundation for everything, can gird us up in its security and strength. What ways have others often tried to "help" us in life? Typically, when we are in a low place, others try to pull us up from some high place, but usually it does not reach and support the depth places in us. But True Love desires to join with us at the very low places and be with us there. Jesus could have come as a King, as Royalty above all that had ever been. But He joined Himself to us in a lowly way, and He still seeks and desires to join with the low and lost places within us. Jesus came to serve in this way rather than to be served.

When we desire to be with the Lord regarding the lost places within us, He has great compassion and love for us there. "I will feed My flock and I will lead them to rest," declares the Lord

God. "I will seek the lost, bring back the scattered, bind up the broken, and strengthen the sick ..." (Ezek. 34:15-16). We rarely have believed that that is really true about the Lord regarding our broken and sinful areas. "When evening came, many who were demon-possessed were brought to Him, and He drove out the spirits with a word and healed all the sick. This was to fulfill what was spoken through the prophet Isaiah: 'He took up our infirmities and carried our diseases'" (Matt. 8:16-17). Similarly, Jesus said (Matt. 11:28), "Come to Me all who are weary and burdened, and I will give you rest. Take My yoke upon you ... My burden is light" (Matt. 11:28-30). Great compassion is evident in these verses. Christ wants to lift our burdens through joining with us in the lost places. He goes so far as to say that He "takes up" our infirmities and "carries" our diseases. Anytime I've heard these verses preached, I've always heard them related to the "final" event of the cross. But here, we see Jesus saying that He carried our diseases *in connection to healing* all the sick people that were brought to Him.

Jesus essentially identified with and absorbed as if His own the sin and the diseases of His people, but because He knew and was filled with the Father's Love, all our infirmities and diseases were dissolved and became as nothing upon encountering Him. Just like with the leper, the uncleanness, sickness, and sin were able to come into contact with Him and the fullness of Love – and they hit a Wall. Sin hit a wall of the light of the presence of God in Jesus. And true Light exposes and dissolves darkness, making it into light (Eph. 5:13). The cross, regarding Jesus taking up our infirmities and carrying our diseases, was not just some final event that occurred in Jesus' natural life, but was a way of walking. He constantly joined Himself with His people's infirmities and diseases in a way that His Love could then touch and heal. The light of the presence of the Lord, when allowed by people to touch them, loved and healed them. However, we have yet to allow the Lord to love us in this way as a whole. We tend to resist the notion that He desires to join Himself with us, be present with us, and to love us especially in the places that are most lost and lacking of His love. If we would but receive Him this way in our own lives such that His love could complete us in the areas that are lost and lacking of His love, then that powerful all-reaching Love would be able to come pouring through us in a way that profoundly frees and heals those around us as well.

While the Lord fervently seeks to love us in the ways described above, our lack of transformation still provides evidence that we likely have unending ways that we hinder Him from joining us. So how do we hinder His joining with us? God makes clear that what we join with, from our end, is critical. "Or do you not know that the one who joins himself to a harlot is one body with her? For He says, 'The two will become one flesh.' But the one who joins himself to the Lord is one spirit with Him" (1 Cor. 6:16-17). Way more than we know, we have joined with the harlot rather than with the Lord. Because of free will, Christ can desire to join with us and yet we can still be joined with the harlot more often than with Him.

How do we know during our walk with the Lord whether we are joined to Him or to the harlot? "For each tree is known by its fruits" (Lk. 6:44). Often, this verse has been used about people in an overall way regarding whether they are believers or not. Rather, this verse is about being able to tell what our walk is like at any given point. Which tree within us is governing us at the moment – the tree of flesh or the tree of spirit? When the fruit is "bad fruit," that is evidence that we are joined with the fleshly, worldly person within us (the "harlot tree") rather than with the Lord (the "tree of life"). When we join with the "old self" or earthly person who is connected to the harlot, we will experience the fruits of anxiousness, frustration, insecurity, and lack of love and peace in general. When we join with the "new self" or with Christ within, however, we will experience the fruits of peace, rest, love, and the fruits of the Spirit as a whole. These fruits are a clear cut way for knowing whether or not we are inwardly joined with the Lord or joined with the fleshly, earthly person.

The core or "inward part of us" that can join with the Lord or with the fleshly person is the soul. People have often been confused about the differences between the spirit, soul, and flesh, however. While the difference between the spirit (the spiritual person) and flesh (the worldly trained person) is clear, the differences between soul and spirit or soul and flesh are not as clear. For example, sometimes people have referred to the soulish nature in us that is very much about our flesh or carnal nature. Likewise, the scriptures very much indicate that the division between soul and spirit is a very deep place of division and can be difficult to discern (see Heb. 4:12). This confusion is because we have not understood the soul.

For clarity, it helps to view the soul as a wineskin (that the Lord said should be flexible) that conforms to whatever we participate with. This wineskin is a vessel; it is who we are but conforms to whatever we join with. When we join the earthly rather than the heavenly, our soul becomes filled with the world and we rigidly cling to the things of the world for a false sense of security. We are not a flexible wineskin when we have conformed to whatever the flesh demands for a sense of security. That is why King David said in Psalm 23 that the Lord was His Shepherd and that He "restores" his soul. After being trained and filled by the world's ways throughout childhood, our soul has conformed to the ways of the flesh and the world. We became "soulish" or fleshly and then had need of the Lord restoring our soul, like David had stated. But as David also conveyed, we are to look to the Lord as our Shepherd who leads us. With our sight and needs fixed on Him, we are changed into His likeness. He restores our soul and the soul begins to conform to the spirit united with Christ within us. So, which is our true identity, the soul or the spirit? *The spirit who is joined with Christ within is the "new name" that our soul is to participate with and eventually fully possess.* That new creation, the spirit joined with Christ within, is our true identity, although we only truly possess that identity as our soul joins with that identity versus the flesh. Then our soul is fully "saved" or redeemed and becomes one identity and one spirit with Christ within.

*Be still; know how fervently the Lord longs to be one-with you, even in your unique places of lack and weakness. Know that Christ desires to keep awakening your soul so as to become one-with Him.*

# Our Part: Joining with the Lord and His Presence through the Way of the Cross

As we continue, you will begin to see more and more ways that we don't join with the Lord. While that may be overwhelming to know in some ways, it will help you learn more about how to participate with the Lord. It will cause you to see the tremendous need for us to pay most attention to one thing in our walk: that is, being in the present moment to be with the Lord's presence. But for now, let's continue to learn more about how we do not remain present with the Lord.

Jesus said (Matt. 13:11-15), "To you it has been granted to know the mysteries of the kingdom of heaven, but to them it has not been granted. For whoever has, to him shall more be given, and he shall have an abundance; but whoever does not have, even what he has shall be taken away from him. Therefore I speak to them in parables; because while seeing they do not see, and while hearing they do not hear, nor do they understand. And in their case the prophecy of Isaiah is being fulfilled, which says, 'You will keep on hearing, but will not understand; and you will keep on seeing, but will not perceive; for the heart of this people has become dull, and with their ears they scarcely hear, and *they have closed their eyes lest they should see* with their eyes, and hear with their ears, and understand with their heart and return, and I should heal them'." These verses have been greatly misinterpreted as God not desiring to heal people. Instead, God's healing is based upon people desiring to see. He would gladly heal them but it requires that they, from free will, truly desire to see and hear. But similarly to what is stated in John (3:19), "Men loved darkness instead of light," here the people "closed their eyes lest they should see." In other words people plainly didn't want to see – because they already liked their lives they had without God. They had no need for God when their lives, although dark and without truth, were satisfied with earthly "riches."

This hardness of heart that occurs when earthly life is satisfying without the Lord is exactly what Jesus faced with many of the Jews. Jesus said to them (Jn. 8:37), "I know you are Abraham's descendants. Yet you are ready to kill Me, because you have *no room* for My word." Just like it was with many of the Jews, we have no room for Jesus' word when we are currently satisfied with our earthly life as it is. We are full of earthly life. We are like a cup full of old water (the old self and life) that has no room for the new. And yet, the new life can only be poured more fully within us when some of the old water or life has been poured out to make room for it. Because we as a people have often preferred earthly darkness to true light, God knew that our only help was the way of the cross being brought into our lives (that of suffering or losing earthly "riches" and ways). Through the cross that strips us of our fleshly, earthly self and identity, our true spirit self and identity is freed. Our true self becomes awakened through the cross freeing us from the fleshly self. Without the cross and thus remaining in our fleshly self and life, what we have is really nothing and will at some point be completely taken away. We can only truly receive riches that last when we lose the earthly life and walk in the new self and life. With that walk, more shall be given.

We who have believed have heard the importance of walking the way of the cross if we truly want to follow Christ. And yet, I can speak for myself that while I have valued walking the way of the cross for many years, until recently I have not known the depths of what the way of the cross has meant at a practical level. There is a deeper way and walk of "losing our life" that we may find true life. Jesus said (Matt. 10:39), "Whoever finds his life will lose it, and whoever loses his life for My sake will find it." Jesus could have stated this in the order of finding true life and then losing our life. But He did not. We are a cup already full of our old life, and that cup must be poured out to make room for true life. That is the cross that is to help us receive true life. That is the cross that is to help free us (although some people get afraid of the imagined suffering when they hear this kind of message about the cross, but I have found that true suffering actually decreases significantly as you learn to walk simply in the present moment).

One of the main ways we suffer is when we experience a sense of separation and aloneness because of *not* walking in the present moment. The reason we experience that separation and aloneness is because we are in the separating, old self anytime we are not present. That is why Jesus said (Jn. 12:24-25), "Truly, truly, I say to you, unless a grain of wheat falls into the earth and dies, *it remains by itself alone*; but if it dies, it bears much fruit. He who loves his life loses it; and he who hates his life in this world shall keep it to life eternal." When we still love our life that is in this world, that is, the old self, we will remain alone and separate in one form or another. But when we participate with the cross by walking in the present moment so as to lose the old self, it dies and our new life in Him becomes freed and begins to bear much fruit. We are no longer alone.

While losing the old life still necessitates the grace of God, the grace is first for losing the old life that will result in an exultation of our new life that is in Him. That is the picture we have been given by Jesus. As soon as Jesus was baptized in the Jordan, the Spirit came upon Him, initially for the primary purpose of leading Him into the wilderness to be tested. The earthly life needed to be tested and found void for the new life to be exulted.

There is deep truth in this spiritual principle of initially losing the old life that will automatically result in true life with no striving needed, which we will see below. But first, let us pay attention to the fact that Jesus described two distinctly different lives when He said about losing one life so that one would be exulted. There is a false life versus a true life that occurs within a person. There is the old self versus the new self, which is essentially a false self versus a true self. One path or way is about holding onto our earthly rights and ways, and the other path is taking up our cross, losing our earthly rights, and deferring to what the Lord's way is. The scriptures say (Phil. 2:7) that even Jesus "emptied Himself" or "made Himself as nothing." Surely Jesus did not make as nothing the Spirit part of who He was. Rather, Jesus did not participate with the desires and rights of the earthly person, the outer fleshly garment. That is the part He emptied so that His True Spirit Person would be exulted and glorified. That's why the scriptures then add (Phil 2:9), "Therefore also God highly exalted Him, and bestowed on Him the name which is above every name." He humbled one life so that the other would be exulted. For us, like with Jesus, God is moved to bestow on us our true names when we have emptied ourselves of the outer garment of flesh.

The Lord's pathway is for us first to lose our old life and self. The only problem is, we as a people seldom walk in a way that loses much of our old life – partly because of an exaggerated fear of suffering, and partly because we don't know how to lose our life or even know how much of our earthly life is not of God. Again, I don't want that you would become fearful or overwhelmed about what all this entails. As we proceed, you will find that being in the present moment with Presence is the way of the cross and will take care of all that we need without our usual earthly effort.

Similar to what has been emphasized above, Jesus made this point about shedding the old life in the situation where His disciples could not cast out a demon from a particular man's son (Matt. 17:21; Mk. 9:17-29). When this man asked Jesus to cast out the demon, Jesus first asked how long the son had been that way. Jesus did not need this information to cast out the demon, as seen by the many other demons He had cast out. Rather, Jesus brought out a point that could teach us something more. When the man had answered Jesus and said "since childhood," we learn that this "demon" was a deep-seated spirit essentially living with the boy his whole life. The demon gained a stronghold because of the impact and training from the world since childhood. This is a perfect example of the strength and dominance of the fleshly mind and all that it gathers along its journey in life. That is the life that Jesus states we are to lose if we are to find true life. That is why Jesus continued teaching His disciples about this kind of demon from childhood (in the gospel of Matthew), "But this kind does not go out except by prayer and fasting." I had always seen this verse previously as about fasting food. But that is not the spirit of what Jesus conveyed here. It is about fasting, starving, or losing the old life so that we can walk in true life.

There are certain ways that we participate so strongly with the "rules," lies, and pain of our earlier earthly life that require serious prayer as well as discontinuing or disconnecting from those "ways" that are continually fed within us. More than we know, we participate with and feed old ways that have been with us since childhood. The Lord, here, with His emphasis on prayer and fasting, encouraged us to pray and especially to discontinue (fast) the ways that strengthen our earthly mind and strongholds. In fact, typically the most important fasting we can do is not regarding food. Rather, it is to fast the old self, the earthly self and all its training, lies, and impact and then we begin to recognize and receive the Presence of the Bridegroom in those places. Jesus said (Mk. 2:19), "While the bridegroom is with them, the attendants of the bridegroom do not fast, do they? So long as they have the bridegroom with them, they *cannot* fast." We cannot fast the old self when the Bridegroom is with us because when He is with us, the old self is not governing us. When the old self is not dominating us, there is nothing to fast. But when the Bridegroom is not present, it is because the old self is dominating again, and fasting is needed. That is especially when fasting is needed, not of food but of the old self. We are full of the old cup trained by the past again, which needs fasted (repented of) so that we can turn again to Christ's presence that is always available when we are in the present.

While recognizing the importance of disconnecting from our old life can seem to place a pressure or burden on us, there is an overall way of walking that automatically disconnects us from the various ways that feed the old self. That is, *learning to be in the present moment so we are available to be with the Lord's presence is really the only thing necessary to keep our attention on in our walk.* This is much of what Jesus was getting at when He said (Lk. 10:41-42), "Martha, Martha, you are worried and bothered about so many things; but only a few things are necessary, really only one, for Mary has chosen the good part, which shall not be taken away from her." Walking in the present moment with the Lord is the simple walk without all the distractions of the world. Paying attention to being in the present moment with Him already begins to disconnect from and not feed the old self and its fleshly mind and ways. Remaining present with the Lord's presence is what causes us to lose the old life that Jesus said we should lose. *Walking in the present moment automatically fasts the old self* because the old self is always in the future or past. That is why walking in the present moment is necessary for disconnecting us from our earthly history and conditioning that usually dominate us. It is a deeper way of the cross. And as we continue to lose the old life, by simply being present with His presence, we will see that we automatically keep finding true life in greater abundance as well. True life and identity simply emerge without any effort as the old self and life are fasted through walking in the present moment with Christ.

When we pay attention to and "watch" our thinking (and emotions), however, we will begin to see that our thinking runs constantly about what has happened previously and about what is ahead. Our thinking tends to dominate and govern us way more than we would believe. Usually, that dominating thinking is so much so that we are often on "auto-pilot" and essentially unaware of the present moment. Most people are rarely truly present. We are, in fact, not really spiritually conscious and aware when we are not present. We review and analyze events that have just happened to make sure we performed well and that people received us well, among many other reasons. Our left hand does in fact pay attention to what our right hand does (Matt. 6:3). It is a paying attention to the performance of the old self, the earthly life, for its glory. When we are very goal driven or looking ahead and maneuvering about the future in some way, it is from fear. We typically use a lens from past impact and try to control our future so that we avoid what the past tells us we need to be fearful of. It is still our left hand paying attention to what our right hand does. All of this is the mind of the old self, the earthly self running and controlling us such that we lose contact with the present moment.

Most anytime we are geared toward the future or the past, we are not in the present with the Lord's presence, and we walk in the old self without grace. Being future and past oriented as a whole *is* the old self. Watch and see how difficult it is to stop the mind from its earthly rampages. We have not lost the old life so as to find true life. The mind, along with the rest of who we are, was meant to serve God. But it has been the other way around. We have served the earthly mind without knowing it. Paul states (Rom. 8:5-7), "Those who live according to the sinful nature have their minds set on what that nature desires; but those who live in accordance with the Spirit have their minds set on what the Spirit desires. The mind of sinful man is death, but the mind controlled by the Spirit is life and peace; the sinful mind is hostile to God. It does not submit to God's law, nor can it do so." In believer or unbeliever, the mind at any given moment that is geared toward the future or past as a whole is the mind of sinful man. It works death; it is the flesh nature or old self that is to be lost so as to find true life.

A large part of the problem regarding staying present is that we have believed that our mind *is* us. And yet, we can see from the scriptures that the earthly mind that has a history of impact from the world is what we are to lose. It is not us, and we are to fast and starve that earthly mind such that the Spirit alone is what moves our mind. Paul said that we are to be "transformed by the renewing of our mind" (Rom. 12:2). How do we renew our mind? By walking in the Spirit we put to death the misdeeds of the body, and we find life (Rom. 8:13).

Walking regularly in the Spirit, however, is impossible unless we walk regularly in the present moment with the Lord's Spirit who is ever-present. Then the Spirit, not us, puts to death the misdeeds of our body. We cannot do that. However, we only have regular access to the Lord's presence when we are present, and when we are present, we will find that He does the work. Only by being in the present moment can we truly be in relationship with the Lord. Only by being present do we have access to what comes with His presence. That is, with His presence comes grace, healing, love, peace, rest, and the fruits of the Spirit as a whole. But we must join with the Lord to be one spirit with Him (1 Cor. 6:17). That only happens through us being in the present moment, with our attention there. As we learn to walk in the present moment with Him just like Jesus did with the Father, that is the way of the cross, and we will find ourselves automatically losing the old life. In turn, we find true life in abundance.

*Cease striving; all striving is striving after the wind and is an attempt to save our lives. Take up our cross and lose our lives by simply walking in the present as our Master walked.*

# Our Part Continued:
## Learning to Be
## Present with Presence

How important is it to be present? It is everything. Can we ever really have true relationship with God when we are not in the present moment? No, it is impossible.

As a whole, we are less able to receive grace from God in the moment when we look back at the past or when we stare at or worry about "our" future. We come out of relationship with Him at those times. In our free will, we turn other directions than to being in the present moment with Him. Receiving grace for our walk, being healed, being girded up during difficulties, knowing we are loved, being able to love, receiving revelations from God, sensing the leading of the Shepherd, and all of the moving powers of God do not happen in or about the past or the future; all of God's power always happens in the present moment. He is the larger than life I AM. And when Moses spoke to the burning bush and asked who he should say was sending him, God said to tell the people, "I AM That I AM." This made clear that there is no real way to describe the Lord. God did not have a frame of reference beyond Himself that could be used to accurately explain Himself to people. "I AM That I AM" is simply the all-sovereign, ever present power that always is. We just don't know Him very well this way because we tend not to walk regularly in the present moment.

The manna in the wilderness was a clear picture of how we are to walk with Him who is present all the time. The people were not to collect any more manna than was needed for the present day. The manna was not just symbolic of food, but of *God's provisions*. In other words, God's provisions are centered on today only and will not be good for tomorrow or afterward. There is no grace and provision for tomorrow or the future as a whole. When we get worked up and anxious about tomorrow and afterward, we are not in the present and are collecting manna for tomorrow, which results in a kind of spoiled provision for us. There's no grace. Christ was the manna in the wilderness and is the provision for us today as well. He said that He would never leave or forsake us. That is about Him always being present, but we can only receive Him and His provisions if we are present in the moment rather than being oriented toward the past or the future. That is why Jesus emphasized (Matt. 6:34), "Therefore do not be anxious for tomorrow; for tomorrow will care for itself. Each day has enough trouble of its own." Do you recognize how almost all of tomorrow thinking and planning is the fleshly, old life dominating us, the life that we are to lose?

When our thoughts are about tomorrow and the future as a whole, they are almost always because of fear. The fear is often connected to trying to control the outcome toward what we think ought to happen (which is typically based on our lens from past history). But the reason we experience fear is because we are "hidden from" our God who is the I AM of the present. He does not know us there, or, as God says in the scriptures, "I do not know where you are from" – because we are at a different place from Him when we are not in the present moment. No wonder we experience fear connected to our imaginings about the future. There is no grace for the future (or when we dwell on the past). God is God of the present and that is where He meets us with His grace. When our minds dominate us and take us into the future or the past, we experience the respective, reactive, and bigger emotions and turmoil because we have no grace. And we have no grace because we are not really at a past place and are not yet at a future time we are concerned about – other than in our mind. Our carnal mind has controlled us. How could we expect grace for being at an imaginary place in our mind? Time does not actually exist for the eternal God because He is always in the present, and He desires that we, too, join Him in the present moment where He and His grace abide. We continually step out of relationship with God when we leave the present moment in our minds. And yet, grace, and the other powers of God, come in the present from the God who is I AM.

When we seek things in the future or from the past it is like that which was said to the women who came to the tomb to attend to the earthly body of Jesus (Lk. 24:5), "Why do you seek the living One among the dead?" This real situation presented in the scriptures is a clear parable for how we walk in life today. When our earthly mind, seeking something to bring us "life" in some way, takes us to the future or the past to do so, it is like seeking something living among the dead. We cannot get anything from the past or from the future because they don't exist at the moment, except as an illusion in our mind. The past and the future are essentially dead to us because they are not present where I AM always lives and reigns. While the past has caused pain that we carry with us, we cannot do anything about the past because it does not exist. If the pain is being carried in us, and is thus still present in us, we can be present about the pain that is there. Being present allows the Lord's presence and grace to be with us such that we can become aware of and shed the lies that the pain still tries to tell us (we will discuss this further later). But when we focus on the past or on the future, we do not have the grace to cope with them because they do not exist at the moment. It is seeking the Living among the dead. And we won't find true life there. It is again like hunting manna on a day different than the present one. We won't find God's provisions. God doesn't allow us to be tempted beyond what we are able at the moment (see 1 Cor. 10:13) even though it feels like it at times; we just give ourselves much more of a load than He intends when we live outside of the present moment. In fact, that is why Jesus asks those who are weary and burdened to come to Him (so as to be present with Him). His load is light – when we lose our load by being present with Him. Suffering is less.

Our goals are important to pay attention to regarding the future as well. If our goals for the future become such an idol that the present only becomes a slave of our all-important future, we are essentially seeking and finding our earthly life – and we will lose true life. We are again seeking the Living among the dead because we are so future focused without knowing it. *When the future is all-important to us, the present is never good enough.* It is a never-ending hole to be filled because the only way for the hole to be filled and satisfied is being content with the present Manna. And when we are present with Manna, we will be led by the Spirit in the moment. But if we bypass the present and keep trying to be satisfied by some future happening, it is death in the end. The manna that we seek and gather regarding "tomorrow" will keep drying up into nothingness, and we will be without True Provision that only ever comes in the now. He is the I AM. When we lose contact with the present moment, we lose contact with Presence, as well as always coming short of finding true life. We are never satisfied with the present moment when we continually treat it like God's provision is not yet enough.

Our minds often wander, usually about future things, when reading a slow book, driving a car, mowing the lawn, hearing an uninteresting lecture or sermon, or doing some menial task in general. These are just a few examples of how much the carnal mind dominates us in life. Even the concept of hope has typically been taught as a future-oriented concept rather than a present-oriented one. False hope is about hoping, wishing, or desiring for something that does not currently exist that essentially causes a "striving after the wind." True hope, in contrast, is a confidence and security about something that does exist, and if anything, it allows a person to be more fully in the present moment because of that confidence. For instance, Christ and the "hope" of His resurrection are not really about some future or past event. The hope of His resurrection is always about now. When we participate with the Lord stripping us of the old self in life through the way of the cross, we can have a constant confidence that He and His resurrection life are presently powerful and available for bringing new life into the empty space made by the falling away of the old. That is true hope. It is a sure hope that is always about now rather than some wishful event in some future time. That is why Jesus said so much about a constant watching and being alert for His coming, as if His coming would happen any moment. Jesus was not trying to get us to stare at some future event. Rather, Jesus' point was for us to be constantly ready for His showing Himself in various ways, especially unexpected and sometimes difficult ways, during our walk. He was after us being very present focused so that we would be able to receive the fruits of His coming regularly in the present moment. That is how we do not miss His coming at "an hour" we do not expect.

Sometimes the old self in people becomes irritated when I mention about not being future focused. It is true that, even when being very present, there will be times that the Spirit will cause us to become aware of something that is approaching – especially when it is something that requires some preparation. The difference is whether or not our mind is working at or fretting about something in the future. When we experience a "striving or working at it" or "can't rest" energy within our mind, that is always the old self with the sinful mind that wants to dominate us. That mind is of the flesh and is always after self-glory apart from Christ. It will exhaust us. When the Spirit initiates something about an upcoming situation or event, however, there is life and peace in how it occurs.

When I have a presentation approaching (for my profession), as the Spirit draws my attention to it, I become present about the topic

I am to discuss. The preparation is more peaceful and effortless than when the mind works at it. The main point to remember about future events, though, is about us truly choosing what we choose. Normally for the majority of people, the old self and its mind overtake them such that they literally made no choice. This is an example of the mind of the old self dominating us such that we serve it (rather than the other way around) when we do not remain present. Even doing menial tasks, we can use those tasks as times to become very present by noticing very clearly what we are doing in the moment. Then we can still be in relationship with the Lord and the time will be rich and satisfying. Or, during menial tasks, we can choose to pay attention to and be present about something else meaningful while doing the menial task. The main point, however, is that we choose to do what we do rather than have the sinful mind dominate or overtake us in a way that makes us vulnerable to its sin.

The other aspect that is important to be aware of regarding learning to be in the present moment with the Lord's presence is that being present does not always mean that you will be consciously in touch with some extra noticeable or tangible touch of God. Sometimes people fervently seek a strong, noticeable touch of God because they lack faith at the moment. Rather, when people are truly in the present moment, they will simply be able to recognize the fruits of the Spirit rather than the fruits of darkness. They will especially sense peace, rest, a security of knowing love, and a desire to love the Lord and others. While God can and does move in some more noticeable ways of touching us at times, people sometimes seek those noticeable touches most when they are in places of fear and lack of faith as a whole. The spiritual principle, here, is that when we are simply in the present moment, God is already present with His fruits of the Spirit. I raise this point because some people get frantic about trying to be present *with the Lord's presence*; they believe that they "should" be able to be aware of the Lord in a constant, distinctly tangible way. While that would be nice, we don't have to be constantly aware in that way. That kind of walk would not require faith. Instead, when we are simply in the present moment (which automatically loses the old life), the fruits of the Spirit will be present and we can trust and know that His presence is always available to us just as He has said: "I will never leave you or forsake you."

If you are fairly in touch with yourself experientially, you can recognize the fruits of His presence that occur within you – noticing when you are at rest and peace and when you are not. Not being at peace is evidence of the old self governing, and vice versa. If we take the issue of expecting God to meet our needs upon being present at the moment, for example, we can sense what our experience within is like, and as a result, whether we are in the old self or not. If it seems arrogant to us in any way when expecting God to meet our needs, that fruit shows us that we are actually in the old self. We are in the past or future about what life is presently like, and we likely have demands or expectations of what life "should" be like. And if it is not arrogance we feel while being in the old self, it is likely a fear or doubt about God meeting our needs – because of looking through the eyes of previous earthly impact. Both fear and arrogance are not fruits of the Spirit and we will experience the dis-ease or lack of peace when such fruits of the old self occur. When we are in the present, however, we will experience rest and peace because we are in a place of simple, genuine trust. When we are in the present moment, we can know God as He is and our expectancy is a soft, secure trust that He will meet our needs as He knows is right and best. We know this at those times because being in the present automatically comes with the grace and fruits of the Spirit as a whole. He never leaves us or forsakes us.

*Be still; let go of the future into His hands and forget what lies behind as well. Accept the moment as it is, even the old self that may be trying to dominate, and let the Lord work into your heart and mind His simple way of being regularly aware of the present moment where I Am is always available.*

# Presence and Identity: Abiding and Becoming One Spirit in Him

Christ is always present and available. That is His part. On our part, as long as we join with Him through the way of the cross, we become one spirit in Him. That is both parts at once, since His part is always available. That is oneness of identity in Him. We addressed earlier that those who join with the Lord are one spirit with Him. Can you get in touch with this spiritual truth at the moment? We can be *one spirit* with the Lord. Pause and be present with that before reading further.

I don't know about you, but for me being one spirit with the Lord is mind boggling. Do you hear that whatever false earthly identity we have maintained has got to fall away? But what is left when the earthly identity falls away? Mostly what comes to mind for people is that the old self falls away and the new self is left. But what is that new self? In the past, without knowing it, I had always viewed the new self as another entity occurring within us that is at least separate and different from the old self – but in my earthly mind, I still perceived Christ within as "additional" to my new self. It was as if we were still two separate entities. However, the spiritual principle that God set up is that those who join with the Lord become one spirit with Him – not two entities but one. That is mind boggling, at least for the earthly mind.

In Hebrews it is written, "'Once more I will shake not only the earth but also the heavens.' The words 'once more' indicate *the removing of what can be shaken* – that is, created things – *so that what cannot be shaken may remain* … we are receiving a kingdom that cannot be shaken …" (12:26-28). What can be shaken? The old life and all that is "created" and not fully God. What is it that cannot be shaken that will remain? Only the mysterious, invisible, incorruptible Presence of God and all that He makes unto Himself will stand. In the light of His presence, when we are present to join with Him, we become as light just as He is light. When we walk in the present moment with the Lord's presence, we keep receiving and becoming one with a kingdom that cannot be shaken. With this kind of walk, we gradually learn that our true identity is an indestructible, incorruptible identity that becomes and is one-with Christ as opposed to the corruptible earthly identity.

Paul, similar to Hebrews, states (Col. 1:25-28) that he was given "a word of God in its fullness" for us – "the mystery that has been kept hidden for ages and generations, but is now disclosed to the saints. To them God has chosen to make known among the Gentiles the glorious riches of *this mystery, which is Christ in you,* the hope of glory. We proclaim Him, admonishing and teaching everyone with all wisdom, so that we may present everyone perfect [complete] in Christ." Wow! What a message that is. Paul felt led to present all people *complete* in Christ. That message is stated such that people have, in a sense, something of Christ placed in them but are not complete somehow. This point makes more sense when we examine the first part of Paul's message. He was supposed to present to people "a word of God in its fullness," that was really about a mystery that had already existed "for ages and generations." While this mystery was only *disclosed* to the saints at this point, the mystery itself had existed for ages and generations. What was the mystery that had essentially always existed? It was "Christ in you, the hope of glory." In other words, Christ was always within people, but people had not learned to participate with Christ.

There are various scriptures that make it clear that the only way to become complete in Christ is to turn to and join with Him. This spiritual truth, however, unfortunately was often taught in much of Christianity in a way that portrayed Christ as only outside us and that He would enter our heart only upon confessing Him. Here, the scriptures point toward Christ always having been within people. In fact, that is how God made us. He breathed His Spirit into us, a portion of His Spirit to each one that cries out "Abba, Father" greatly desiring to be joined in full again with the Godhead. That is what is to happen in the end. The bride, meaning the various portions of Spirit, or Christ within, is to be joined together with the Bridegroom. That is the "coming of the Lord." It is a spiritual joining or gathering together in Christ.

Through the shaking of all that can be shaken, only the indestructible portion of Christ within each person that people have participated with will remain, which is our true identity as we have joined with Him in one Spirit. Isn't it clear that, if all that can be shaken falls away and we remain, we (not the old self) must actually become fully transformed into the indestructible Christ identity? That transformation is simply us losing the old life and identity through the way of the cross such that the new self and identity can finally emerge. This is our soul uniting with the portion of Christ placed within and "possessing" who we were always meant to be. And this transformation and way of the cross most occur through walking in the present moment with the presence of the Lord. It is primarily a "letting go" of the often-dominating earthly life that is typically in the future or the past. It is the Way that Christ walked before us. It is the way of "participating with the divine nature so as to escape the corruption of the world" (2 Ptr. 1:4). This Way of walking in and possessing our true, indestructible identity is simply being in the present moment with Presence, which is a deeper way of the cross that loses the old self and life.

During this process of learning to be present, however, it is good to remember that walking in the present moment is not fully in our control like we often want things to be. While we so often cause unnecessary suffering to ourselves through not being in the present moment, the Lord allows suffering for His purposes. Through suffering, God always births new life, especially when we participate with Him in it. Through suffering, God gives us a wisdom and oneness with others regarding their suffering. And through suffering, God frees our true identity by helping us to let go of (and humble) the old self more fully. Working humility into us, even by the Lord *not* providing the grace for us to walk in the present moment at times, is central for us being able to become a more complete vessel for His purposes. That is why we are not to strive to become present.

God is much larger and all-encompassing than the portion of Christ placed within us. He is within and without. The fullness of Christ is not in our individual body alone. Christ's fullness is eventually to be demonstrated in the whole body of Christ on this earth, each one allotted a portion as the scriptures say. If our participation with Christ within was all that was needed and was to be under our full control, however, we would again lean toward the separation and self-glory of the old self, just as the old self always tries to do. As such, the Lord sovereignly works life so that we are occasionally placed in positions where we cannot walk in the present moment very well even when we want to. That "humiliating inability to be in control of everything" causes us to have to rely on the fuller body of Christ on this earth and on He who is more encompassing than the portion of Christ placed within us. While our deeper, true identity that is in Christ is one with all, His fuller strength and goodness beyond that which is within come through humility, for the scriptures say about humility (Jam. 4:6), "He gives a greater grace." That is why the Lord temporarily leaves us in perceived places of lack at times. In His greater wisdom, He knows that when the old self begins to dominate such that we become more self-contained and separated from Him and His body, we need the help to again see our need and oneness with others' struggles. This perceived place of lack within us, then, causes an awareness of the fragility of the human condition as well as a greater reliance on He who is all-sufficient so that we are able to receive love and to love others from a place of humility.

You will also experience other times of temporarily losing presence in spite of trying to pay attention to being in the present moment with the Lord. Sometimes this kind of "draining experience" will occur for up to several days. Don't let this discourage you in your journey of learning to be present with Him. For example, there are times the Lord "withdraws some of Himself" from you in ways to pour further into others, and for no logical reason you feel significant lack in your walk with Him on a certain day. You can see this kind of experience occur in the Song of Solomon (3:1-2; 6:1-3) when the bride experiences agony because of the Bridegroom's presence seemingly not being available when gathering other brides (lilies). This is what occurs practically at points when you have gained and remained steadfast in new spiritual ground, and, then, on a given day for no apparent reason you find no grace for walking that way.

At these times of perceived lack, because we are one body and one spirit, the Lord takes of Himself from one place and gives to another in need – just like when our physical body brings more healing energy to a bad knee, for instance. The rest of the body and especially the other leg feel a strain as more help is being poured into the bad knee (or whatever area has need). Like Jesus said, sometimes one sows and another reaps (Jn. 4:37). That is what happens at those times, but it is a further building of the kingdom. In fact, because there are relatively few people that really abide in the present moment with Christ at this point in time, we who are awake and present are used by Christ to pour further into others that can leave us depleted after a time of being poured out. As this spiritual season continues and more people learn to become present and awake, however, abiding in the present moment will become easier and those who are awake will experience fewer forces hindering them from remaining awake. As we remain faithful in the difficult times and humbly stand fast in belief that Christ is still doing much kingdom work during these periods of the cross, we will continue gaining ground and being renewed to even greater fullness in Christ. The sacrifice is well-worth the kingdom life being further built on this earth. I have always experienced greater insights, revelations, and new life following a time of the cross.

Taking into account that the Lord temporarily allows places of perceived lack on our part, we are not to give up regarding paying attention to being present with Him. Rather, when we have unsuccessfully attempted to let go of the earthly distractions so as to simply become present with Him, we can ask for His greater grace for seeing His will in our situation. His will may be to humbly ask so as to become present, and yet in His sovereignty and wisdom He may either grant or withhold that grace for His greater purposes at that point in time. If He does not give the grace to be present, His will may be to pray for others from that position of "lack." Praying for others when we are deeply in touch with that place of need is a tremendous prayer that prays from a place of humility. It is much like Christ joining us in the low places to gird us up at those places.

Many times, our own places of nonpresence and earthly suffering that seem to have no grace are especially the times that God desires prayer from us on behalf of others who suffer similarly. Just like Daniel prayed, we can confess our own sin and then pray that the sins of others as well in those ways would be forgiven (really meaning removed). That is powerful prayer. But the important point about being "unsuccessful" in regaining presence in particular situations is that we must allow for God's rights and wisdom when regaining presence seems not to be in our power at the moment. We are to "accept the moment" as it is, which includes accepting ourselves. As we honor and accept the moment and ourselves, we will find that it is not very long until we see the

Lord's greater wisdom and purpose for not immediately regaining presence. Likewise, we will soon find the grace for becoming present after we have let go, accepted life as it is, and joined with the Lord's purposes.

*Cease striving and know who you are when you abide in Him. Be present and quiet for a little while about knowing who you truly are in Him and that all else will gradually be shaken away.*

# The Upright Will Dwell in Thy Presence

The psalmist exclaimed one of the more fundamental spiritual principles for walking in the Spirit when he said (Ps. 140:13), "The upright will dwell in Thy presence." When we are present, we are finally able to dwell in His presence, and we are also more able to experience His goodness on our behalf as well as on behalf of people He connects us with. Dwelling in the presence of the Lord, when we are not concerned about future or past, is a place of trust in Him rather than in the flesh. "He who dwells in the shelter of the Most High will abide in the shadow of the Almighty. I will say to the Lord, 'My refuge and my fortress, my God, in whom I trust!' For it is He who delivers you from the snare of the trapper, and from the deadly pestilence" (Ps. 91:1-3). This place of trusting the Lord and being present with Him, even in the face of difficulties, is the place of Mount Zion. Mount Zion is essentially a finished Jerusalem where the Lord does battle for us because everything is turned over to Him as seen in the following scriptures: "… the Lord Almighty will come down to do battle on Mount Zion and on its heights" (Isa. 31:4); and, "Those who trust in the Lord are as Mount Zion, which cannot be moved, but abides" (Ps. 125:1). *When we are present, that is the proof of our trust in the Lord*; it is the proof of our abiding in Him, which results in Him (and His riches and fruits) being allowed to abide in and be available to us. He battles and works on behalf of us when we are in the present moment that shows our trust in Him.

When we pause for a moment regarding how Jesus walked this earth, we can recognize how He constantly abided in the present moment with the Father. Even when the Pharisees, demanding an immediate answer, brought to Jesus a woman caught in the act of adultery, He did not get flustered with worry about where all of this was heading. He remained present, pausing and writing on the ground with His finger while the Pharisees kept persisting on getting an answer from Him. I am convinced He was very present regarding the situation, but being present with the Father as well – and the grace was available for a beyond-human answer when it seemed to us that there could be no good answer in that kind of predicament. That is truly abiding and being in the present. Being present like that definitely requires trust in God.

Dwelling or abiding in the Lord is a spiritual truth that was restated by Jesus many times with His disciples. "*If* you abide in My word, then you are truly disciples of Mine; and you shall know the truth, and the truth shall make you free" (Jn. 8:31-32). Because Jesus never leaves or forsakes us in life and is always present in all of our circumstances, *if* we trust Him and lose our life during our circumstances and simply become present with Him, we will know the truth of His word and the truth will set us free. To abide in Him and His word is to be present with Him while not saving our lives during the various circumstances, and we will be surprised at His saving grace.

In one particular longer passage Jesus came across somewhat repetitive with His disciples: "Abide in Me, and I in you. As the branch cannot bear fruit of itself, unless it abides in the vine, so neither can you, unless you abide in Me. I am the vine, you are the branches; he who abides in Me, and I in him, he bears much fruit; for apart from Me you can do nothing. If anyone does not abide in Me, he is thrown away as a branch, and dries up ... Just as the Father has loved Me, I have also loved you; abide in My love. If you keep My commandments, you will abide in My love; just as I have kept My Father's commandments, and abide in His love. These things I have spoken to you, that My joy may be in you, and that your joy may be made full …" (Jn. 15:4-11). Jesus emphasized a somewhat intertwined abiding in each other in a way that is much like our earlier discussion on true identity. He portrays it in a way that sounds like it is hard to distinguish One from the other. That is our being present with His presence. He earnestly desires to join with and abide in us in the difficult and lost places, but we have usually distrusted Him there and left the present moment. Usually, with our mind taking over from fear about the future as viewed through a lens from the past, we bail out of the present and neither abide in Him nor let Him abide in us.

Christ desires to *abide* in us. What a thought. With Him abiding in and being a noticeable presence in us, we are bound to experience the support, love, and grace to deal with whatever difficulties come along. This simply shows how much we do not allow Him to abide in or have His presence honored within us (although He is always within us).

The scriptures say (1 Cor. 13:13), "But now abide faith, hope, love, these three; but the greatest of these is love." The word "abide" was specifically used here because it conveys that these heavenly riches always remain; they are always present – because the Lord is always present. He never leaves or forsakes us. We have simply "not had access" to Christ and these steadfast ways of His because we have not remained in the present moment in our walks where He and His unshakable ways and riches continually remain. When we violate the present moment that is in accordance with His whole I AM ever-present nature by our being oriented toward the future or past, we take ourselves out of the present realm and out of relationship with Him. When we are not in the present, we cannot be in relationship with the Lord. And we cannot have true and accurate learning about life without true relatedness with Him. That is why our abiding in and being very present in the moment with Him is critical. When we are present in the moment with the Lord's presence, we can relate more accurately with Him and more accurately with whatever we presently encounter. When we are not fully present in the moment, our carnal mind with its lens from past history is virtually always distorting our sight of "what is" at the moment.

Dwelling with the Lord in the present moment, then, means honoring whatever moment is before us. Honoring likewise means accepting the moment as it is. *Unless we first honor and accept the moment as it is, we cannot have true relatedness with, and thus, accurate learning about, "what is."* Any internal resistance takes us out of the present moment. Any internal resistance to the present moment places upon the moment expectations and "shoulds" or "shouldn'ts" (usually based upon a lens of past experiences) that orient us more toward a "world" that does not actually exist. In doing so, we essentially treat the Lord like He is not present and was not sovereign regarding the present circumstance. We treat Him like we know better than Him regarding what life should be like at the moment. As soon as we have demands about what our situation should look like, we bow to some idol rather than to the Lord who is sovereign. When we have demands about life, we have no true relatedness to "what is." We cannot truly learn about what is, or about what the Lord may be working the moment for. While the earthly event may be what we consider "bad," we can never respond to or even see the moment accurately unless we are first present to be with the Lord's presence and grace, as well as present so as to be awake to the actual circumstance. True learning, and thus godly responding, can only come from true relatedness to what is. That only occurs when we are present in the moment and not resistant to what is.

In Hebrews, it states (12:14-15), "Make every effort to live in peace with all men and to be holy; without holiness no one will see the Lord. *See to it that no one misses the grace of God* and that no bitter root grows up to cause trouble and defile many." Here is a great example of a passage that ties together some very important points. We can see that God emphasizes the importance of not missing His grace. In other words, His grace is available but we could still miss it. How do we miss His grace? His grace comes from being in the present moment where His provisions are, and when we resist the moment or step out of the moment and "into time," meaning the future or the past, we can miss the grace of God. God being eternal is not simply life that doesn't come to an end. Eternal has to do with "not in time" because He is always present. He simply always IS. We are to become like Him. We are to come out of "time" and abide regularly in the present with Him. Then we do not miss His grace. And when you look at the above verses again, you can see that the warning about not missing God's grace is central for being holy and living in peace with all men. When we continually honor and accept the present moment as it is, rather than resist it, we do not miss the grace as well as the other provisions of God (His holiness, rest, peace, etc.). But when we step, instead, according to time (future or past) or according to our own expectations and we leave the present moment, that is the old life always ready to take over with its earthly lens from the past that can quickly cause "bitter roots to grow up, causing trouble and defiling many." Any resistance to "what is" in life creates unseen bitter roots – which Jesus did not walk in.

Part of dwelling in and honoring (rather than resisting) each moment in life with the Lord means humbling yourself in His presence. James stated (4:10), "Humble yourself in the presence of the Lord and He will exult you." Humbling ourselves in His presence is crucial, and it is about a way of walking, not just a one-time event. Two lives are shown here again. One life or self is to be humbled and one life or self is to be exalted. When we lose faith and then the earthly mind works to control the events in the present or for the future, we have not at all humbled ourselves in the presence of the Lord. When the mind governs us like that, it is always fear based and is rooted in our own efforts toward gain, or, to avoid certain things we have already experienced in the past. It is in the realm of time and comes from the old self raising up to control life again. Anytime we leave the present moment to find provisions other than what God has sovereignly worked, all of it is hardness of heart. All of it is a trap that hinders us from being available to receive the Lord's grace and goodness. When we do not participate with the old self and its schemes, however, the old self is humbled. And the only real ongoing way for that part to become humbled is to learn to walk in the present moment rather than turning toward the future or the past as a means of earthly familiarity, security, control, or gain. Then, we will find true life. Then, our true self or identity will emerge. That is when our true self, the portion of Christ within that we have finally joined with, will be exalted. One self or life is exalted because the other is humbled.

Part of being humble means not acting on our own initiative, just as Jesus did nothing from His own initiative (Jn. 8:28). The first place we see peoples' separate initiative being dealt with is when the flaming sword was placed at the entrance of the garden of Eden, which we will see more about in a moment. People have sometimes interpreted that passage as God not wanting or being able to be with Adam and Eve anymore because of their sin. Rather, this new season of life occurred *for* Adam and Eve because, without it, they would have handled life just like we do when our old self and life have enough earthly riches to go on our merry way without God. That is exactly what happened initially in the garden. All things were good, and they stepped in a way that turned from relationship with and trust in God. Adam and Eve didn't fully trust the Lord and His provisions as they were as seen by the way the serpent easily tempted them.

The serpent made it sound as if God wasn't really out for their best interest when He withheld the fruit of the tree of the knowledge of good and evil; and Adam and Eve, then, distrusted the Lord and took their own initiative. That distrust was what caused their own initiative to stretch out their hands and eat of the apple. Do you see? From the very beginning, even before eating the apple, Adam and Eve must not have truly known the Lord and His love as shown by their belief of the serpent's lies about

God. They simply had finally demonstrated not knowing God's love when they ate the forbidden fruit. When their eyes had been opened and they saw their nakedness, this was simply them finally becoming aware of their sin and lack – which was really the shame of their nakedness of not truly knowing (and being clothed in) the Love of God. But stretching out their hand "to take" the forbidden fruit was from their distrust of God. Distrust was the origin of sin. Aware of Adam and Eve's distrust and the resulting impetus to "take for themselves," God then implemented something new (Gen 3:22-24), "… lest he stretch out his hand, *and take also* from the tree of life, and eat, and live forever — therefore the Lord God sent him out from the garden of Eden, to cultivate the ground from which he was taken. So He drove the man out; and at the east of the garden of Eden He stationed the cherubim, and the flaming sword which turned every direction, *to guard the way to the tree of life.*"

God created us to dwell in His presence. He created us to be in relationship with Him, and He knew that relationship and our knowing Love could never occur through distrust and taking. So the Lord set up a spiritual principle such that we are prevented from receiving the fruits of the tree of life when we take for ourselves or step from our own initiative regarding life. This is our earthly striving in life, which comes from distrust. Jesus never stepped from distrust and His own initiative. For the majority of us, however, that is often untrue. When we step from our own initiative and try to take, it is because of distrust. When this happens, we lose contact with the present moment and become energized by energy that is not of the Spirit, and this "taking" shows up in various forms – striving, controlling, maneuvering, pressuring others, or undergoing unhealthy emotional reactions connected to not getting what we think ought to be. These things are not of the tree of life.

One of the most significant ways that we "take" rather than trust the Lord during our walk has to do with when sin or imperfection becomes evident in our lives. The majority of people on this earth, even faith filled people, tend to be unaccepting of imperfection and sin within self (discussed earlier in chapter 4). We don't truly know that the Lord accepts us where we are, and from that distrust, we try to take. Our earthly, old self and its energy show in many ways at those times – judging, hiding, maneuvering, getting angry, striving, and so on. When the old self rises up and takes initiative because of not accepting imperfection and sin within self, it becomes a downward spiral. The tree of life is guarded by a sword when our own initiative takes over, and, as a result, we cannot find rest or peace.

The peaceful and life-filled fruits of the tree of life, in contrast, can only truly be received when we walk in a way of trust. Being accepting and regularly honoring of the present moment at hand, which includes accepting self with sin and all, demonstrates that trust. It is the way of the cross, of acceptance and surrender of the present moment. The way of the cross is a losing of all of our earthly agendas and simply being present in the moment, and through this way of the cross we will find that His initiative does move us with grace – in His time. The tree of life and all of its life-filled fruits are regularly available to us when we are simply present. That is when we demonstrate trust. But when we distrust and strive from the old self with its lens of the past skewing the moment as well as the future, the flaming sword prevents us from receiving of the tree of life.

*Be still and abide in Him rather than "take" because of distrust. Be still, trust, and abide in His tree of life within where all grace abounds – even grace enough to work all things together for good in spite of unwanted sin.*

# Being in the Present Moment is True Worship and True Seeking

Only when we are in the present moment are we in true relationship with the Lord. Only in the present moment do we truly worship Him who is I AM. Only remaining in the present moment is abiding in Him and displaying our trust of Him. As soon as we leave the present moment, we in essence bow to something or someone else. Leaving the present moment reveals that we don't believe that He and His presence are enough for us. It demonstrates that we aren't satisfied with His present provisions and that we find it necessary to look beyond Him and the moment to find those provisions. That is why we will experience continual discontentment in the moment when we are regularly future oriented.

When we live in the old self and life by walking in the realm of time (future or past), our treasure is of the earth. We serve mammon, or earthly riches, rather than God. *The old self's overarching goal of separateness for self-glory can only be achieved by leaving the present moment where God is.* The old self cannot stand in the present moment where the light of truth is, so even when seemingly focused on the present, it will be through a lens of the past that maintains its separate identity. More often, though, the old self is striving toward some future place with supposed greater self-glory, still for the purpose of achieving separateness that can only be found outside of the present moment. When we truly desire to "simply be" with no agendas and thus abide in the present, however, we are (without even trying) already present with the Lord who is always present. Then we find heavenly treasure that money can't buy. Jesus, when stating these spiritual truths to His disciples, spent much focus on illustrating the importance of being like the lilies of the fields that are not concerned about anything. They do not strive but accept God's present provisions. The lilies worship God simply by being as they are, and they are then truly present with Him. Everything, like the lilies, was meant to worship God. Jesus encouraged us to be like the lilies, not worrying about tomorrow or about what we wear. Instead, we are simply to be present.

What do we seek? If we are serious about seeking the kingdom of heaven, which Jesus told us to seek first and that all else would be added, then it means being serious about walking in the present moment where the Lord reigns. This would mean paying regular attention to whether or not we are actually present in all that we do. This awareness can only be done through watching and noticing whether or not we are present. Watching is significant in our walk (which we will see more about later). That is why Jesus emphasized (Matt. 6:22) "The lamp of the body is the eye" early in His discussion about paying attention to where our treasure is and what we worry about. The eye is for watching. And it is critical what our eye is focused on, just as Jesus warned about throughout these passages.

Jesus explained how critical it is to watch whether we are seeking earthly or heavenly treasure (which is the old life versus true life). He emphasized this when He added to the notion of the lamp of the body being the eye (Matt 6:22-25), "If therefore your eye is clear [single], your whole body will be full of light. But if your eye is bad, your whole body will be full of darkness. If therefore the light that is in you is darkness, how great is the darkness! No one can serve two masters; for either he will hate the one and love the other, or he will hold to one and despise the other. You cannot serve God and mammon. *For this reason* I say to you, do not be anxious for your life, as to what you shall eat, or what you shall drink; nor for your body, as to what you shall put on." When our eye is bad, it is when the old self is trying to control life because it is concerned about separating earthly things or treasures for self to promote self-glory. When Jesus exclaimed "for this reason," He clearly pinpointed our normal, common worries of life that cause us to have a bad or dark eye. While we may consider normal worry and trying to control things for the future as no big deal, those things are still about us having a bad or dark eye. And Jesus stated that if our eye is bad, our whole body is filled with darkness – and further, if we treat those dark ways as light, how great is that darkness. We simply underestimate the destructiveness of treating ourselves like it's no big deal striving or being geared toward the future; and yet it is one and the same with our whole body being filled with darkness. It is the old self. Why is our whole body filled with darkness? It is because we blindly allow the old self to reign freely as if there is nothing wrong with it; we act like it is light. The darkness is greater than we know when we call darkness light. No wonder our lives feel empty, unsatisfying, and exhausting when we seek in the way of racing toward future directions.

We simply have much further to grow in understanding that, when we are future focused (because of worry and self-glory), it is the old self dominating us again. It is the earthly treasure and darkness we still cling to without knowing it that leaves us empty in the end. Only as we are convicted of the darkness of bowing to future concern, rather than to the Lord, will we ask for His help in letting the future go and abiding in the present with Him. Lord, have mercy on our blindness about how we turn from relationship with You when we become more concerned about the future than You.

Our typical concern for the future versus how Jesus was fully in the present is seen when His disciples desired that He would go to the upcoming feast and show Himself to the world. Jesus stated that (John 7:6), "My time is not yet at hand, but your time is always opportune." When Jesus said "your time," He meant their earthly time. When the old self governs and sees good, earthly rationale for doing something, we take initiative and do it rather than patiently following God's initiative as Jesus did with the Father. That's why "our time," our earthly time, is always opportune. Jesus' time, however, was not yet "at hand." That meant that God the Father and His presence at hand had not initiated that action on Jesus' part yet. Only after everyone went to the feast did Jesus attend. Had He been dishonest? Of course not. A little while later, Jesus' time, because of still remaining in the present with Presence, was in fact "at hand," and He went to the feast. Jesus' "time" was only through the present moment. Time didn't really exist. Only the present was of focus to Jesus. While He was aware of the future through the Spirit, He continuously remained in the present with what was at hand. That is why Jesus said that His "time" was either "at hand" or "not at hand." He only dealt with the present.

When John the Baptist and Jesus preached, saying "The kingdom of heaven is at hand," they meant that the kingdom was somehow present and that the people should be alert to what was happening in the present moment. However, the people as a whole didn't know what was meant by "at hand." The whole way of functioning in the world up until that point was only through the false or old self. The old self is future or past oriented, and even when it is present oriented, it still views the present moment through a lens of past earthly history. So when people discussed and focused on life issues, even heavenly issues, it was almost entirely in a "box" of future or past. They had great discussions about what was to come in the future and great emphasis on what the past would say about the present and future, but the present moment in its own right didn't really exist for people. That is still our tendency as a people today. That is why those around John the Baptist and Jesus would not have understood the expression "The kingdom of heaven is at hand." The many parables of Jesus emphasizing the importance of "watching, being alert, or being awake" because of not knowing the "unexpected hour" of the coming of the Lord would not have made sense (see Lk. 12:39-40).

Even today, the majority of believers tend not to see the full truth of what the above scriptures point toward. The "hour" that we are to be alert for is not an hour or future time like we would normally think. Because the old self still tends to dominate most people, we likewise still focus on future or past just as our ancestors have. So beware, "lest the master come suddenly and find you asleep" as Jesus said (Matt. 13:36-37). Jesus' emphasis on being alert, awake, and watching is about becoming truly awake in the present moment such that the old self would die. Jesus' warnings are about the need to be present focused rather than how we usually focus. As the old self dies, along with its focus on time (future and past), we become awakened to being in the present moment with true Presence that makes all things new. We become awakened to the present moment such that we join, bow to, and become one spirit with Presence so that all else begins to bow.

As we regularly bow to true Presence through walking in the present moment with the Lord at hand, we worship Him in spirit and truth. We become joined with Him in one spirit, and we become one nature with Him. All that can be shaken will fall away, and all that remains becomes and is the indestructible. We posses our new name and our true identity by partaking in the divine nature that escapes the corruption of the world. Let us be present and truly worship the Lord rather than worshipping the world. Let us seek first the kingdom which is always at hand, and then all else that is necessary will be added.

*Cease the striving of the old self, which is always about separation for self-glory. Rather, be still; be present that your worship and relationship unto Him is a pure offering.*

# Being Present:
# Master of the House

Have you experienced trying to hold a conversation with a person who was distracted and was focused on something else at the moment? I know that I have. I first found myself talking to myself, then stopping communication, and then gradually waiting to see if the other person would notice that I had stopped talking. I could tell that they were "inaccessible" when they were so absorbed in what they were distracted by. When their focus was so much another direction, there could be no "relationship" with me at that moment. And yet, in those situations, you or I will typically allow free will and let the other person focus on what they choose to focus on. That is God with us. Generally, the Lord allows free will and lets us focus where we do, even if that means we are not really accessible and in relationship with Him.

Accessibility, through being present, is crucial in our walk with the Lord. If we, the true master of our house, are not present, it is in a sense an empty, waterless (Spiritless) place and many unclean spirits can dominate the house (Lk. 11:24). Our bodies of flesh are simply houses or vessels for holding and emitting forces of darkness or forces of light. And if one is not present, the other will be. Said another way, if light does not take its rightful place or position within us, then darkness will. But God wanted that light would shine forth out of our dark vessels of flesh. That's why Jesus spent so much time talking about letting our light shine before men (Lk. 5:15-16). In fact, Jesus emphasized that our light was meant to shine and that it was not to be put under a peck-measure. Here, Jesus refers to our vessel of flesh. Our vessel of flesh, while actually containing the light of true Presence within us, could result in simply being a peck-measure or covering that essentially hinders all light from shining before men. Whether or not the light is hidden or free to shine really depends upon whether or not we participate with the divine nature within us or with the old self, the earthly self. When we participate with the old self, our true identity is essentially not activated within us and it's as if we are not present within our vessel of flesh. The master of the house is not truly home. While that true identity is still inside the whole time, it is essentially a light hidden by a peck-measure. That is why it is so important for the new self, our true identity, to be present and awake in our body of flesh so that light can shine. When our true identity is present, light is shining and unwanted spirits must leave.

Every time we are not present, however, the spirits joined to our old self can keep reentering the "house," finding it "unoccupied" and "swept and put in order" (see Lk. 5:15-16). In other words, these returning spirits have a house the way they like it for doing what they want to do (put in order), and when they reenter, they not only return but they bring along other spirits more wicked than they are. This explains why some "disorders, diseases, and mental and emotional struggles" seem to increase over time. We, the true masters of our houses, have not been present and have allowed the old self and its accompanying spirits to become present and govern (to fill the void that is available within our vessels of flesh); and as such, those spirits become the masters of our houses – at least for substantial amounts of time during our walk when we are not truly present. The word "swept" is also used in the above verses regarding a house that is unoccupied. Anytime the word swept is used in the scriptures, it is used in connection to some kind of destruction that sweeps away like a flood wiping out what lies in its path. Lord, help us to be present. Help us to learn to be present that we would not allow a void within us for unwanted spirits to govern. Help us to become the true master of our house that we were meant to be, the master that is joined in spirit with You.

"For we know that if the earthly tent which is our house is torn down, we have a building from God, a house not made with hands, eternal in the heavens. For indeed in this house we groan, *longing to be clothed with our dwelling from heaven*; inasmuch as we, having put it on, shall not be found naked" (2 Cor. 5:1-3). I initially saw these verses as about some building in heaven in some future time. Rather, when these verses are viewed as pertaining to our old self with the flesh "house" versus the new self that is joined in one spirit with the Lord within as the heavenly dwelling, they begin to make more sense. We are exhorted in the scriptures at various points to put on clean garments, white robes, and our heavenly dwelling so that we would not be found naked. That kind of exhortation is for now, not in some future time.

Can you see that when we merely participate with our earthly, old self and the fleshly body as our home, we are still found naked? And, that this normal earthly "light" is still really darkness? We are not the master of our true house at those times. Only as we become clothed with the divine nature within do we become clothed with our dwelling from heaven. That dwelling is indestructible. Only then are we not naked and truly clothed. This clothing, as mentioned in the verses above, is our house not made by human hands. It is spiritually built from within by conforming to Christ. We are to be built up in Christ. Paul fervently worked in the strength of the Lord so that Christ would be formed (built up) and brought to completion in all people. That clothing is the portion of Christ we were made to be but it can only be possessed to the extent that we turn to and join in one spirit with Him. Only as we are present and joined with the divine nature within are we truly being master of our house. Only then do we keep strengthening in or gaining our heavenly clothing, our true house. When we learn to walk in Christ's way of the cross, a way of trust rather than a way of taking, we become clothed in this true identity. We become clothed in knowing the truth rather than being deceived by the lie that we are the insufficient false self. The false self strives while the true rests in belief that "God is", and as such, there is no insufficiency or lack. God's provisions are seen as enough, and we know we are true sons and daughters.

Jesus said (Jn. 8:35-36), "And the slave does not remain in the house forever; the son does remain forever. If therefore the Son shall make you free, you shall be free indeed." We can see in these verses the old self that has been a slave governed by the enemy while in our house (or vessel of flesh). That slave will not be allowed to remain forever, but like the tares sown among the wheat will go to destruction at the time of harvest (Matt. 13:24-25). The true son that walks in the present with the Lord's presence, however, will always remain in the house, enjoying the freedom of that eternal house that is beyond the restrictions of the realm of time. Also about our "houses," Jesus said (Mk. 13:15-16) "And let him who is on the housetop not go down, or enter in, to get anything out of his house; and let him who is in the field not turn back to get his cloak." This statement is similar to the peck-measure illustration Jesus used. When we have joined with our true identity and have truly begun to shine as the master of our house, we are in a place of praise and worship of God. It's as if we are bright shining lights on our housetops, or, really, lifted high and spiritually shining atop our vessels of flesh. Jesus makes clear that we are not to go back and "enter in" and get something out of the house again, meaning we are not to go back into the old self that is earthly. When Jesus adds, as well, about not turning back to get our cloak when we are out in the field, He is referring to those who become harvest laborers in the "fields" that are white for harvest. He is exhorting those harvesters not to turn back to put on their earthly cloak or old self again.

When we are present and truly master of our house, we are a gate for light to this dark world. Our words, prayers, gifts, and actions are empowered by the Spirit when we are present for the Lord's fruits to come through us. When we are not present, however, we are a gate for darkness often without knowing it. In this case, our words, prayers, gifts, and actions will not produce the Lord's fruits, but rather, fruits of darkness.

Gates are where everything happened in the Old Testament. Battles were won and lost at the gates. That is still true. The present moment in time is like a portal or gate where one thing or another takes place. Dark forces or light forces prevail at the gate of the present moment. Likewise, our souls are our gates that can open up to those forces of light or forces of darkness during each present moment. At the gates of our souls, we are to take all thoughts captive to the obedience of Christ (2 Cor. 10:45). That is our powerful spiritual warfare. That warfare is effective warfare when we watch at the gates in union with Christ. In fact, Christ *is* our gate when we watch in union with Him. The psalmist said (Ps. 118:19-20), "Open to me the gates of righteousness; I shall enter through them, I shall give thanks to the Lord. *This is the gate of the Lord*; the righteous will enter through it." The psalmist indicated, during the midst of difficulties and discipline, that he would enter into righteousness, the place of heaven, of Christ, through the gate of the Lord. This gate is Christ's gate and is about Him doing battle on our behalf when we simply watch at the gates of our souls in union with Him who is within us. When we are not present and watchful with His eye of Spirit, we fail to see what He sees and we become vulnerable to darkness.

In union with the eye of the Spirit, however, we are able to see the thoughts and emotions of the fleshly old self that are not us. We see their schemes to dominate us, and we are able to discontinue participation with them. Then, having let Him be our gate, we are truly able to enter and abide in Christ and His rights. In Ezekiel (46:1) we can see that the gate of the inner court was only open on the Sabbath. That is a clear picture of rest. When we are present and watchful in union with Christ at the gates of our souls, we are able to enter the inner court, the place of rest and peace as well as the place of Christ's rights that battle any foes for us. And when Christ takes ground back from the fleshly mind or old self within us, He has established Himself along with us on that "land" within us. He has given us that land like He said He gave to Jacob when Jacob dreamed about angels ascending and descending on a ladder that reached to heaven. That ascending and descending is representative of a holy way, a "roadway" or land, which can be regularly traveled by the Lord and all His angelic workers. That is a "house" of the Lord as well as a gate of heaven to this earth that is referred to in Genesis (28:17). But that land or holy roadway can only be gained within us when we watch with the eye of Spirit at our gates so that the Lord can keep taking new land. That is why Jesus said (Jn. 10:3), "The *watchman* opens the gate for him [the Shepherd], and the sheep listen to his voice."

What happens at our gates? What happens in our present moments? Do we truly realize how important the present moment is? Eternal is always now. There is no future or past; only now always exists spiritually. When we become awakened to this, we begin to walk as the eternal beings we were created to be, coming out of the realm of time and walking in each present moment. Then, we walk as the scriptures say to walk, "Pray unceasingly." When we regularly walk in the present, we become alert to "what is" at the gate of our being, and we only open the gate in response to our Shepherd's voice. But the gate is only opened by the watchman, one who is present and awake. The presence of our faithful Shepherd, then, melts away and transforms into light all that is not light. All the earthly elements are to melt away, even now as we participate with the Lord in a way that was always meant to be.

Being present and alert and "one-with the Lord's eye of the Spirit" is prayer and worship that continually bring transformation through the light of His Presence. That is a gate of heaven. The Lord governs through people who, through free will, are present with Him such that His light keeps working to cause all to bow.

That is how we are to pray unceasingly. That is our warfare that destroys unwanted earthly fortresses that have seemed impossible to destroy. All of this spiritual power, however, only becomes present and freed to work through us to the extent that we remain the master of our own house by being in the present moment. When we remain the master of our house and joined with the divine nature within, the light of His presence continually works to cause all things to bow to Him.

Simply by being present and peacefully watchful, even when we are not fully consciously aware of the Lord at the moment, *allows* (because He is ever-present) His eye of Spirit and therefore His sight to be the lens we look through in the present. When we are not present, and therefore not master of our house, however, there will automatically be unwanted spirits governing our house as well as the lens of what our eyes see (just like how the scriptures (Mk. 3:11) say about the evil spirits within people seeing Jesus and bowing – the people were not present and the spirits governed them). When we are not present, we will be in the old self and under its evil spirits and their lies about the present, past, or future. But if we are truly present or awake in a given moment through being peacefully watchful, it will be the eye of Spirit that sees with and for us such that we see with a clarity regarding what is. Being truly present causes us to be deeply aware of our own thoughts, feelings, actions, and life as it is whereby we become a more spiritually informed, awakened vessel in how we handle life – as opposed to being governed by unconscious actions that can hurt one another.

*Be still, and be, so that you, the master of your house, would not be absent and have your house broken into by thieves. Only when we lack presence and are essentially unconscious do we do violence and harm to the world and those around us.*

# Watching at the Gates:
# Key to Abiding in the Present

"The lamp of the body is the eye" and is therefore key to watching at the gates. When you think of a tall lamp stand with the lamp at the top, that is like our body with the lamp of our eyes at the top. In other words, with that tall lamp stand, where does all the light come from? It comes from the lamp that is placed at the top. With us as people it is the same. The eyes are the lamp where all the light comes from in our walk. When watching from the position of Spirit and the light comes out through our eyes, where is the light coming from? It comes from Christ within – as long as we are watching in union with Him. The Psalmist says (Ps. 18:28), "For Thou dost light my lamp; the Lord my God illumines my darkness." While the Lord can illumine our darkness and be our lamp, we still have free will. For example, we can watch by being aligned with Him, where He is our lamp, or, we can watch through the eyes of the sinful mind with its thoughts and emotions governing all we "see." The eyes are crucial and are made for watching. That is why Jesus placed so much emphasis on watching, being alert, and being awake. Will we watch in union with Christ and see Him and His provisions in our situations, or, will we see with the sinful mind and perceive constant lack in our earthly situations? When we watch in union with Christ, we will experience the fruits that come with His light. When we watch through the eyes of the sinful mind that has been trained by the world, however, we will find that the light that is in us is darkness, and how great that darkness and its fruits will be.

Learning about our struggles or trauma areas can help us understand the distinction between watching with the Spirit and watching through the eyes of the sinful mind that brings death. When someone has negatively impacted you in a significant way, especially if it is a way that you have already experienced much pain about previously, what kind of watching takes place? Invariably, you watch outwardly – to protect yourself from getting hurt again. That is normal, and yet, it is the old mind that wants to dominate us and keep us separated from knowing the love and security of God. Watching outwardly is almost always driven by fear and the old self that tries to save itself. Watching outwardly with concern is a clear signal that we are in the old self. That is when our eyes are dark and we cannot see clearly. The sinful mind puts a distorted slant on everything – and how great is the darkness for us and the others around us.

Watching in union with the Spirit, however, is about watching inwardly. Jesus said (Matt. 22:37), "Love the Lord your God with all your heart and with all your soul and with *all your mind*." God's works to produce love within us and through us are inward not outward works. The scriptures also say (Matt. 6:23), "If therefore the light that is *within* you is darkness, how great is the darkness." We can only discern that darkness within by watching inwardly. Likewise, the scriptures state (1 Ptr. 4:7), "Be clear minded and self-controlled *so that* you can pray." None of our godly works, prayer or otherwise, are truly godly unless the inside of the cup is first clean and initiated from a pure place at the moment. Some people begin getting concerned when raising this point of paying attention inwardly because of all the futile pursuits by psychology's analyzing and digging into past history. This watching that Jesus emphasizes, however, is not at all about the past or about analyzing, digging, or judging what is seen. Rather, the watching referred to here is about a restful, peaceful watching as the true master of our house such that unwanted spirits do not take advantage of a house where the master is not present.

When the watchman watches at the gates in union with the Spirit so as to catch the sinful mind and its tricks to take us out of the present moment, it loses power in the light of our Shepherd's presence. All that is exposed by light becomes dissolved into light. That is what the lamp and the watching are to catch. We are to catch the darkness of the old mind that tries to blind and govern us. Remember, the sinful mind of the flesh that has been trained by the world is always opposed to God and wants to dominate us. It wants to keep us out of the present moment and under the distortions of the past as well as the fears about the future. If it is able to keep doing so, the old mind keeps being needed. But we are to take *all* thoughts captive to the obedience of Christ (2 Cor. 10:5). That's a lot of watching, but it is okay when it is done from a present, peaceful place. And the more we catch ourselves not being present, we have not failed those many times but have gained in overall presence through each instance we have caught ourselves.

We are to be transformed by the renewing of our mind rather than being conformed to the world and its rules, limits, and expectations (Rom. 12:2). That can only be done well by abiding in the present moment, and abiding in the present moment can only be done well by watching in union with the Spirit. When we watch in union with the Spirit, we can catch at the gate of our soul all that is not of the Spirit. When we watch being aligned with the Spirit, we have a clear, single eye as the scriptures say. The single eye is us being in union with Spirit, but the dark eye has many distortions (and distractions) of the old self and its earthly history of pain. Medical doctors that have researched and studied the eye have found that, with a particular instrument for examining the eye, they can see various shades and colors in the eye that are connected to various kinds of pain and trauma still present from childhood. That is having a dark eye rather than a clear or single eye. While some doctors still study the eyes in this way (referred to as Iridology), this was common practice by many doctors until about the last 50 years or so.

When we watch in union with Spirit, we can sense a more pure watching. While watching around the room you are in, say to yourself, "I am watching through my eyes." Notice what you experience as you keep watching through your eyes and being aware that you are watching through your eyes. Do you sense the purity of that watching?

Invariably, people experience a greater richness when watching like this, partly because of simply being very present when watching. But the richness comes from more than simply being present. When you watch this way while sensing a pureness, who is watching when you watch through your eyes? Unless you are watching outwardly at someone who has just impacted you, it is not the old self watching through your eyes. It is you joined with the Spirit. It is you partaking with the divine nature within who is watching. Christ and His Spirit are within you. When you say to yourself "I am watching through my eyes," you are watching from within. *When you watch from deeper within, you watch in union with Spirit. You watch in union with Christ.* And when, from that position, you watch the mind and its thoughts and emotions, you begin to see that the thoughts and emotions are *not* you. Thinking that thoughts and emotions are us is one of the biggest lies of the sinful mind that has allowed it to dominate and control us throughout life. Because we experience our thoughts and emotions physically in our body, especially our emotions that send electromagnetic waves throughout our body (discussed later), we typically believe that they *are* us. When we believe this, it makes us helpless victims to their rampages. We think we have no choice but to go along with their futility. However, the thoughts and emotions of the sinful mind that have come through the training and impact of the world are of the old self. They are not us, and yet we have fallen for the lies that they are us. When we watch in union with the Spirit, however, we finally begin to see the thoughts and emotions as distinct entities that live in our body of flesh.

In fact, I have found it helpful to consider the old self's thoughts and emotions as "things" within me that are not me. As I consistently see and talk about them as things, I am more able to separate myself from them and feel less like a victim to them. They are no longer part of my true identity, but rather, nuisances that try to deceive me to leave the present moment into an illusory world. As I join with the Spirit in watching, I keep growing in joining with my true identity and leaving the old one behind. Watching is partaking with the divine nature, and that identity and nature increase while the old identity with its lies and chains begins to dissolve by the power of the Lord's light and presence.

Watching *is* being present. When in union with the Spirit we watch the old self and its thoughts and emotions that are caught up in future or past, that is being present. When we watch, we cannot watch *and* participate with the old self in the future or the past. We cannot participate with Spirit *and* the sinful mind. When we see the sinful mind working at something toward the future because of fear, it dissolves quickly because we stopped participating with it when we became present to watch it. It also dissolves into light because watching with the Spirit brings the light of the Lord's presence upon it. It is important, however, that we do nothing about what we see. We are not to judge, criticize, or analyze anything because that would be the old self coming in another way that makes judgments about "what is." When we simply and restfully join the Spirit in watching, the light and the love of the Lord's presence begin to melt away all the earthly elements.

When first learning about watching the thoughts of the old self, someone else suggested that I try to watch my thoughts for several moments. Why don't you try to do that as well for a few moments, from a relaxed watchful place with the Spirit before you proceed.

Did you find that you didn't get to see any thoughts? That

is what usually happens. The more you watch, the less the mind of the old self governs. When you watch from the eye of Spirit, the thoughts of the old self cannot stand or dominate as they normally do. If when you tried to watch, however, you did notice various thoughts entering your mind, you were likely already joining with the old self more than truly watching with Spirit. Likewise, when you watch from the old self position, you usually watch for how you have performed. That is a self-conscious kind of watching through the eyes of the old self that is about performing for acceptance or self-glory. It is the old self working for a better, separate earthly identity in some way.

Some people, upon learning about the importance of being present and watching, become fearful about not "succeeding" in this kind of walk. That is the mind of the old self trying to have them stare at the future already. It shows how powerfully the standard of performing has been trained into them during life – as well as the unacceptance experienced when they do not perform well. Recognizing that you have just been in the future again, however, even many times, is already gaining ground in the present moment because you cannot "catch yourself" about that unless you are present. Noticing whenever these lapses into the future or past occur is a watching and being present that gains spiritual ground in you. Catching yourself is always victory, so don't judge yourself. Just notice. *Love reveals but does not judge.* Also, if we have encountered some kind of difficulty or trauma, we often lose contact or consciousness with the present moment. The way back to the present moment is simply to begin watching within from the position of Spirit again to notice the happenings within us. Even if we are unable to gain consciousness enough to watch until after difficult events, presence keeps gaining ground while the old self loses ground.

We were made to be present like the trees, birds, and the lilies. They have no mind and therefore no choice, and yet they simply give glory to God by being what they were meant to be. That's the way we were meant to walk in life. We were meant not to make our own judgments and choices apart from God but to trust Him to express Himself through us like the lilies. That's why the way of the cross is so important in our walk. It's to let go of our judgments and choices such that we live in the present like the trees, birds, and lilies. While it's clear that we were made to be present, like Jesus walked before us, we typically find that we have come out of the present before we know it. What, then, is necessary for staying in the present? Watching. Watching with the eye of Spirit, more than all else, is essential to abiding in the present, and therefore, the Lord's presence.

Watching at the gates is really one of the (if not the) most important disciplines – as much as reading the scriptures daily, fasting food, or even prayer – because watching is necessary so that prayer comes from a place of belief, peace, and love rather than from the unbelief, fear, and manipulation of the old self and its mind. "Be on guard, that your hearts may not be weighted down with dissipation and drunkenness and the worries of life, and that day come on you suddenly like a trap; for it will come upon all those who dwell on the face of all the earth. But keep on the alert at all times, praying in order that you may have strength to escape all these things that are about to take place, and to stand before the Son of Man" (Lk. 21:34-36). The scriptures emphasize (2 Tim. 1:14), "Guard, through the Holy Spirit who dwells in us, the treasure which has been entrusted to you." We guard, honor, and defer to the Holy Spirit and the portion of Christ placed within when we watch so as to remain present.

We see this critical emphasis on watching when "the hour of darkness" was upon Jesus and His disciples in the garden of Gethsemane. Jesus had previously emphasized to His disciples (Jn. 14:27), "Let your hearts not be troubled," which would come from the mind of the flesh trying to deceive them about God's provisions not being what they ought to be. Here in the garden, then, Jesus acknowledged to His disciples that His own heart was troubled and that He was sorrowful to the point of death. Drinking of the cup that the Father placed before Him is the only issue in the scriptures where we find Jesus' heart being troubled. Likewise, this is the only place we see Jesus powerfully wrestling with the Father's provisions. In the end, we learn that Jesus accepted the Father's provisions and that He therefore came to a place of peace again. But what Jesus said to His disciples tells much about how He got through to the place of peace again. "And He came to the disciples and found them sleeping, and said to Peter, "So, you men could not *keep watch with Me for one hour? Keep watching and praying, that you may not enter into temptation; the spirit is willing, but the flesh is weak*" (Matt. 26:40-41).

Do you see Jesus' emphasis on watching and praying? He said to *keep watch*. In Luke (12:35), it is written, "Be dressed in readiness [alertness and watchfulness], and *keep your lamps alight*." Now, in the garden Jesus said "Could you not keep watch with Me for one hour?" in a way that indicated that one hour was minimal because watching was to be an ongoing way that all of Jesus' disciples were to walk in life. Jesus also emphasized that the watching was not to be outward but "that *you* may not enter into temptation," especially at a critical time like it was in the garden. The watching was to be inward. Do we really watch regularly like this in life, especially at critical times so that the mind of the old self does not overtake us? Jesus' emphasis with the disciples is likely what He Himself emphasized in His own walk to get through what He had to get through in the garden to come to a place of peace. We typically do not walk with that kind of watching in our life. No wonder we often have unwanted spirits taking residence in our house that has no master present. That is exactly what happened to the disciples when they did not keep watch as Jesus had.

When we watch from the position of the Silent Watcher, the single eye of Spirit, we will see the folly and darkness of the thinking and emotions of the sinful mind within our body of flesh. We will see the deceptiveness of the old self that is in bondage to the things of the earth, and we will see that that is not us. Paul said (Rom. 7:20), " But if I am doing the very thing I do not wish, I am no longer the one doing it, but sin which dwells in me." When we begin to separate from the old identity, we will see and join further with our true identity (which is one spirit with God). We will also see the sin that has so easily entangled us, but we will see that it is not us. We will become more of our new name that is of Him rather than of the world.

Being watchful and present disidentifies with thoughts and emotions. Watching from a restful place with Spirit is not about detaching from thoughts and emotions psychologically as if they don't exist. That is the main way historically that people have tried not to let the emotions dominate them, but it is still the mind of the old self trying to do it. That way is still about psychological defenses trying to control life without experiencing it. Being fully present, in contrast, is not "cutting off" and denying the reality of emotions. Rather, it is about being present enough such that you are very much paying attention to, aware of, and even experiencing the emotions and the thinking but now are able to see them as not the real you anymore. They are not you. They are entities of the old self and not the true you when they govern and control you beyond what you will or desire. And when you are aware of them and see them as the old self that is not you, that is disidentifying with them (which is different than detaching). Watching at the gate of your being in this way is remaining master of your house. That is why Jesus said (Matt. 13:24-25), "The kingdom of heaven may be compared to a man who sowed good seed in his field. *But while men were sleeping*, his enemy came and sowed tares also among the wheat."

*Be still; be watchful of your inner state and its fruits. When you notice fruits from the old self, and thus its darkness, do not judge, resist, or try to change what you notice. Simply noticing makes you present rather than feeding or participating with any darkness or wickedness that proceeds from within.*

# Watching Body Pain: Burning Away the Tares

The old self, just like Satan, can mentally know and quote certain scriptures and yet not truly bow to and know the Lord in those areas. *Our freedom is not so much based on what we mentally believe but on how present or conscious we are in life.* For instance, we can know or "believe" that we are loved one moment, and then in another when the old mind has taken us on a ride under a lens of fear, we have no clue that we are loved. Freedom is not as much about belief as it is about being present, for when we are present, belief is then present and accessible. Freedom from unnecessary pain and suffering comes from being freed from the mind of the old self and its lies that cause us not to be present. And being freed from the power of the mind of the old self does not come through striving or trying to believe more than we currently do. Freedom from the mind of the old self only comes through being present and watching with the eye of Spirit so as to remain present. When we remain present and spiritually awake, the mind of the old self cannot unknowingly overtake us like a thief.

Throughout our lives when we were "sleeping" (not spiritually awake), the enemy sowed tares within us. The tares are essentially the false or old self and its lies that are of the world. The old self grew through the training and negative impact of the world, and its sower, or parent, was the enemy. One of the most destructive forces within the old self is body pain – emotional pain and its attached thoughts that we carry within our body from previous negative impact. Body pain and its respective thinking and emotions are powerful tares sown among the wheat. Have you had a significant other simply say one particular statement to you and you feel thousands of electric zaps rush immediately throughout your whole body? And if you are less prone to experiencing emotions, have you experienced your whole countenance change immediately by one certain comment from a close significant other? Unless you are completely cut off from emotions and your inner experience as a whole, you have surely experienced these experiences. That is body pain that has been stored up within the flesh. It is a powerful entity used by the old self, much like the thoughts and emotions of the old self as a whole, except far more powerful.

Research bears out the powerful mind-body connection and its toxic thoughts and emotions that often govern who we are in life (or, really, the false self we have often perceived ourselves to be). One source that you can read to learn more about this area is "Who Switched Off My Brain?" by Christian medical doctor, Dr. Leaf. Thoughts create electrochemical reactions within the brain. I'm sure you're aware of the many chemical imbalances that people live with in life. This research provides greater evidence of how thoughts, especially ongoing patterns of certain thoughts, create chemical imbalances. Then these chemicals essentially produce electromagnetic waves throughout the body. The electromagnetic waves are either healthy or unhealthy depending upon the thoughts we have. Thoughts, especially constant patterns of thoughts, that are in accordance with the old self and its body pain will send electromagnetic waves that can even cause structural damage at the cellular level within the body – hence, sickness and diseases such as migraines, arthritis, diabetes, strokes, heart problems, and cancer. In other words, patterns of unobserved destructive thoughts begin to take over our bodies in various kinds of ways. I believe that mental and emotional disorders, sicknesses, and diseases as a whole originate through the old self and its sinful mind, and in particular, through body pain. That is why the scriptures say that the sinful mind produces death.

Thoughts that originate from the Spirit, however, produce true life and peace, as well as the other fruits of the Spirit. In this case, we will experience healthy electromagnetic waves that maintain and even heal or restore health. This research evidence about what kinds of thoughts we have and their respective consequences demonstrates why we must be serious about "taking all thoughts captive to the obedience of Christ." Some patterns of thoughts, in particular, are powerfully destructive as seen by the body pain that we carry within us.

Body pain is emotional pain from previous negative impact stored in the flesh that intends to be on the alert for any possible similar impact that it might encounter. You've heard the term "self-fulfilling prophecy"? That is true here. Body pain expects to, and does, see what it believes it will see. In fact, it vehemently works to prove what it already "knows" to be true. Because body pain is part of the fleshly old self, it doesn't forgive or forget even if we have already consciously forgiven the person that inflicted the pain. This pain lies dormant within the body and is always watching for further potential impact and, often without our awareness, it subtly communicates and acts in ways that greatly increase the likely recurrence of some aspect of the negative kind of impact it has known. Then, anything that appears remotely similar to the original impact immediately triggers the enormity of this pain. Typically, significant body pain is experienced much like trauma. The pain that has been carried within the body has been a tremendous load, and it is terrified of that deep well of pain getting touched again. And when it does get touched, much of the original trauma is re-experienced – typically at the expense of an unsuspecting onlooker (usually a significant other).

Significant others are typically the ones that seem most to retrigger people's body pain and trauma, but it can be various life situations or events, or even "God." The reason this pain is so substantial, however, is not because of significant others, life events, or God. Rather, it is because body pain is just that – body pain. My point is that, because it is pure pain that resides in the body, it has *no* other lens whatsoever. As an entire entity of pain alone, it has no balance of good and bad experiences. They are *all* bad. That is why communication, when governed by the body pain and its related thoughts, is all or nothing communication.

When we are in strong body pain, we will find ourselves seeing things as someone "never caring for us" and "always being hurtful and thoughtless" and so on. We define and view ourselves entirely according to that familiar, painful identity that is all from pain – and no wonder Jesus said how great that darkness is when we do not see through a clear or single eye. Body pain never has anything good to say. It is a never-ending well of darkness and death that can never be satisfied – because it is all pain and sees no possibility of anything else because it hasn't experienced anything else. That's why it has no hope. And when we are on the receiving end of body pain that is communicating through someone else, we hear those unfair and unjust all-or-nothing words toward us that put us in an all-bad box. We experience from the person the never-ending pit that can never be satisfied. They don't just happen to say they were hurt about something, but the hurt will sound as if we personally devastated them beyond repair in a way that we can never be forgiven. We either become defensive, responding back through our own body pain, or we shrivel up under the weight of believing the lies that that darkness communicates to us. But the body pain is easy to discern because it comes from the separating, old self and communicates messages of separateness, messages that always separate one person from another.

Couples frequently find themselves in disagreements that seem irresolvable because body pain sometimes governs most of their communication. While each person's words may say one thing, the body pain speaks much louder and more forcibly than the actual words. In fact, on the receiving end it can feel like the communication is somewhat vicious, accusatory, and belittling when the other person believes they simply communicated firmly about their points. This unsettling experience, however, is because the body pain is selfish and doesn't forgive. It doesn't ever want to re-experience the pain that it has already endured and will do just about whatever it believes is required to stop the "enemy." And that is just it, when we look outward and see or treat the other person with a watching paranoia or fear, we are deeply under the lies and influence of the body pain we carry. Everything is distorted so that we can only see the bad, which is typically not nearly as bad as our dark eyes tell us that it is. We only see the bad because that is all that the body pain consists of – pure pain from bad experiences, often from childhood and what we have subtly worked, evoked, or at least participated with in our current relationships. The trouble is, the significant other is not the enemy. The "wickedness" proceeds from within, as the scriptures say.

The various aspects of body pain are tares that had been sown within our souls when we were not spiritually awake. Even if a significant other has substantial body pain of their own that impacts you significantly, focusing on them never brings restoration. Even if your points are thoroughly valid, there is no way out by focusing on the other person. The only way to restoration is through watching with the eye of Spirit your own body pain so as to begin dissolving that pain (which we will discuss further below). That kind of watching burns away the tares within us. You will find that once you begin seeing the truth rather than looking through a dark lens governed by the body pain, you will be strengthened and be able to take new steps that further free you as well as your partner. For example, in more extreme or abusive situations, when you watch the body pain within yourself, you become more freed from it, which finally allows you to take healthy space from any abusiveness (and that "new life" within you, in turn, begins to help bring new life to the person who is more abusive).

Underlying the violent outbursts and abusiveness is unacceptance of imperfection and sin. The most significant body pain that seems nearly impossible to dissolve is unacceptance of imperfection and sin (as addressed in chapter 4). When unacceptance of imperfection and sin within self is powerful, the Lord will typically not grant freedom from the unwanted sins *until* we first learn acceptance of imperfection and sin where we currently are. Again, we cannot perform or attain this. Striving will do no good whatsoever. And even with me emphasizing messages of not striving, those who are powerfully under unacceptance of imperfection and sin will still tend to receive messages like these in this book as tasks needing to be performed by them. When unacceptance of sin is the core issue, the Lord will essentially expose and uproot this area by leaving you "stuck" in a place of seeing your sin over and over – with Him desiring for you to simply agree with Him over and over that you are to be loved and accepted where you are in spite of your sin. Even if it takes a year or longer to learn that crucial lesson, that is a lesson that He requires of you before you are able to mature further in your walk with Him. Without you learning to receive acceptance and love while certain sins are yet unchanged, you will not be a steadfast, faithful vessel or messenger for others of His deeper love that never fails.

The body pain that is centered in unacceptance of imperfection and sin is the deepest one to break. That is usually the core of the old self. When that "pain" of unacceptance becomes broken, however, the power of the old self is broken and you become aware of the Lord's power and love at a personal, experiential level. You begin shifting in an overall way from a vessel using mostly earthly power to one of heavenly power.

If this issue of not accepting imperfection and sin has been your personal stumbling block, don't strive to change it. Instead, ask the Lord to help you learn and receive His love that accepts you in spite of your sins. Even more, simply "agreeing with the Lord" about acceptance and love in those sinful areas should be your primary, if not only, place of focus for as long as that season takes. Focusing on other lessons will simply distract you from your most critical lesson that brings initial freedom. Only after the lesson of accepting imperfection and sin is learned will other lessons seem more accessible to you. For then, that powerful body pain of the old self will have been broken and humbled. In addition, upon accepting imperfection and sin you will be able to remain in the present moment more fully – for unacceptance of self immediately takes you out of the reality of the present moment.

As you continue to watch this phenomenon of body pain as a whole, you will see that body pain plays out way beyond that which happens between individuals. In-group and out-of-group dynamics occur very similarly: one family with another, one cultural group or race with another, or one religious group with another, as just a few examples. When one group criticizes or judges another group, that stems not from love, but from body pain with earthly eyes. An earthly eye cannot see itself and always looks outward and notices things about others rather than self. That is body pain governing. Body pain will show itself through a fear or paranoia, level difference, judgment, and staring outwardly regarding others, even if seemingly motivated by trying to walk righteously. Watching with the eye of Spirit, however, we are able to pay attention to what occurs within self so as to clean the inside of the cup first. The Spirit is always about taking the log out of our own eye before attempting to "love" or reprove our brothers or sisters when we perceive them to be in a less-than-desirable place.

As you pay attention to body pain in life, you will notice that masculinity and femininity play a role in expressing and dealing with body pain. The feminine characteristics tend to be an advantage in becoming aware of emotions and body experiences at a more subtle level. We must become more fully aware of our emotions (rather than being detached emotionally) before we can really watch and learn about what is truly occurring within us. We can "think" we are at one place and actually be at another, but our emotions are a response to our inner thinking and actually demonstrate the thoughts or beliefs deeper within us. As such, it is valuable for us to be aware of our emotions even at a subtle level. The disadvantage to the feminine characteristics is that being so utterly in touch with emotions can take us for a ride when the emotions are heightened. Women as a whole tend to be more in touch with their emotions in a way that can significantly overwhelm them. In these overwhelming situations, they tend more toward losing significant contact with the present moment when body pain is ignited.

The masculine characteristics, in contrast, tend to be a disadvantage when we are unaware of the various emotions and experiences occurring within – for we must be able to be aware of and learn from what the emotions show us about what is happening within. That is being present and aware of what is. Men, in general, tend to be more on the end of being unaware of their experiences and emotions (I have heard women refer to this as the "missing gene" in men). However, the advantage of the masculine characteristics is that when body pain gets ignited, men tend to be more able to maintain contact with the present moment and with what is true – at least cognitively. For instance, they may say the words regarding what is true, but the body pain within them may govern significantly at the experiential level – showing that the truth is not fully known after all.

When you find yourself in "familiar" disagreements, the body pain is usually governing the entire communication on both parts. Communication, even if seemingly present focused, is likely all tied up in the past and, hence, the dismal future. Typically, neither of you are truly the master of your house at those times. You have lost contact with the present moment and unwanted spirits are allowed to reign. Often, you may have felt no hope about these areas of pain between the two of you ever getting resolved. As mentioned earlier, that place of no hope is because the body pain only knows the bad and has only ever known the bad. Because it is pure pain carried in the body, and only has a lens of pain, it likewise can never know anything different. So in its world of all that is known and can be known there is no potential for anything new or different in the future. Communicating further, when still under the influence of body pain, only confirms both person's pain and bad experiences with each other. Both persons' versions are strengthened because neither knows that all of it is an illusion. As mentioned earlier, not being present and, therefore, not being truly conscious, is what causes violence and harm to one another in this world. If we were truly awake and conscious, and in touch with our true identity, we would not dream of hurting one another.

When there is an inability or unwillingness to be in a learner position on both persons' parts, that is clear evidence that body pain is dominating. Non-learner and body pain are one and the same. The only way out of these places is to acknowledge that body pain is governing all the communication with a dark lens that only seeks to confirm all the "bad" about the other person as well as all the bad ways that we define self. Only when we take space and fast or discontinue communication through body pain and learn to watch those dark entities within self do we finally begin to recognize the chance for freedom from this dark bondage. Only then can we begin to see and receive the other person with a love that is from God. Only then can we begin to define ourselves in His light and goodness. Still, this is a process.

Jesus walked on this earth in a way that saw people through the eyes of love rather than through the darkened eyes of body pain. Jesus said (Jn. 14:30), "For the ruler of this world is coming, and *he has nothing in Me.*" Jesus had no body pain stored within Him because He constantly forgave the world as He walked. He had no expectations of what should be but rather accepted people and life as they were. Jesus didn't define Himself by certain peoples' actions or "bad" life events. Because Jesus was spiritually awake and alert, the ruler of the world was able to gain no ground or bitter root in Him. Jesus did not react to people from His own pain because He carried no pain.

We, in contrast to Jesus, carry the pain of unforgiveness in our body. When we are asleep spiritually during negative impact from others, we typically define ourselves according to the way we were impacted. Defining ourselves in destructive ways that do not leave us is much of the ongoing pain and power behind body pain. If our voice was treated as if there was nothing of value, we define ourselves as if we have nothing worthwhile to say. If we are treated like we don't matter, we define ourselves as worthless. Those are tares getting planted by the enemy "when we are asleep." Jesus said (Matt. 15:13-14), "Every plant which My heavenly Father did not plant shall be rooted up. Let them [the Pharisees] alone; they are blind guides of the blind. And if a blind man guides a blind man, both will fall into a pit." These verses shed light on what happens when a couple tries to communicate through their body pain that has been planted by the enemy. Because of the falsely planted body pain that produces a lens of blindness, both persons fall into a pit – a pit of darkness.

How do we watch in a way that begins to dissolve the body pain? As was mentioned previously, the first thing *not* to do is to watch outwardly. That is an earthly eye that cannot see itself. When you can tell that you cannot stop yourself from watching outwardly at your significant other, space is needed. When you watch outwardly with a lens of fear, paranoia, or anger, it is all the poison of the "wickedness proceeding from within." It is the enemy working through the body pain of the old self, prowling around like a roaring lion waiting to devour someone. That is why it is always important to take space during these times such that you are less prone to staring outwardly. When you take space you can begin to watch with the eye of Spirit. You can watch for any thoughts that keep trying to dominate you, or you can simply notice and allow yourself to experience the pain that keeps occurring in your body. Whatever you watch or notice, do not fight it or judge it. Harshness towards yourself only feeds the energy of the body pain. Even if the pain is somewhat intense, as you simply notice it you will see that it will begin to lose power – especially when you begin to notice that it is *not* you but an entity within you that wants to govern you. It is an entity that has gotten away with doing what it does without your consent.

For me, when the body pain feels more intense or overwhelming, I have found it more worthwhile to simply notice the pain.

Sometimes I feel it all through my midsection and chest and other times I have noticed it in other parts of my body as well, like my knees and toes. When I do nothing at all about the pain other than to keep noticing it, I sense it dissolving and losing power fairly quickly. For me, I tend to experience the dissolving of the pain much like a melting into love. Along with that experience, without trying to think about or work at anything other than to watch, the revelation comes to me, "Oh, you [the painful area] haven't known compassion or love!" That's probably the essence of what I have experienced the most connected to those dark places of pain within me – a deep awareness that that place had not known love. But it is not just the awareness about that place not knowing love. I literally experience that place melting into love. And once I have come to a place of peace and knowing love in that area, then I turn my attention to the entity or "thing" in the other person and watch from a place of the Spirit. What typically strikes me there, as well, is "Oh, that place in them hasn't known compassion or love either!" What I find, even without any communication or contact, is that the body pain in the other person has either dissolved or greatly lessened in strength. Likewise, I find that I don't use the other person (really, their body pain) as a faulty standard at the moment because of seeing with the eyes of Spirit. This is the scriptures in Galations (6:1-2) coming true: "Brethren, even if a man is caught in any trespass, you *who are spiritual*, restore such a one in a spirit of gentleness; each one looking to yourself, lest you too be tempted. *Bear one another's burdens*, and thus fulfill the law of Christ." These scriptures are not about believers versus unbelievers but about whether someone is spiritual versus earthly in the moment. The trouble is, we all too often try to restore others when we still have a log in our own eye.

When watching with the eye of Spirit, however, the Lord's light dissolves body pain within ourselves or in others wherever the watching is focused, as long as we are clearly at a place of watching in union with the Spirit. While major body pain in both significant others is not likely dissolved fully even after several times of watching (because it was usually built up over a life time), you will find that it loses significant power after each time of watching with the Spirit. You will recognize the body pain's loss of power by the amount you become able to stay present in those situations. In other words, you will keep gaining ground in the amount you are able to stay aware of what is happening rather than losing complete consciousness or contact with the present moment because of body pain dominating everything.

One other struggle regarding remaining present at the onslaught of body pain is when the body pain is more subtle. For example, there are times I knew I had just experienced a bit of irritability or anxiousness within my body from some kind of interaction with someone. But sometimes the feelings immediately disappeared and as I watched, I could see or sense no thoughts or emotions. Later, I had realized that the pain that had "disappeared" had just hidden. It was still there but just wasn't noticeable enough to watch. Part of what had happened, as well, was that I wasn't watching at all with the eye of Spirit but through the darkened eyes of body pain already (earthly eyes that cannot see self). In essence, I was more joined with my earthly identity and old self than with my true inner identity that is one-spirit with Christ.

Since learning the above, I have recognized that part of watching when the body pain and its thoughts don't seem noticeable in me, first and foremost, is to pay more attention to joining with my true identity than to noticing any of the old self's entities within me. This means primarily paying attention to identity or who I really am at the moment. For example, I am not the earthly person with the earthly name that I and those who know me think I am. That is all earthly. That is all the outer identity of the old self with its earthly roles. My true identity, in contrast, is the unseen spiritual body of light that fills the vessel of flesh. My true self is one-spirit with Christ. As long as I am clear on whom I am and then watch in union with Christ and my identity in Him, I will not unknowingly watch through the darkened eyes of body pain. *Being well-grounded in our true identity in Him that is spiritual is critical to loosening the grip of the old self and its body pain.* This definitely takes much practice that will usually happen through both trial and error.

At times we will be caught off-guard and not recognize that we are in body pain or even that we are watching through the eyes of the body pain. Allow for the process of growth and for God's grace for gradually growing this discipline. He, in fact, allows the mishaps to bring about more significant learning. Sometimes we want everything to be fully under our control and for books to tell us that everything should be able to be under our control immediately. That is the old self again wanting life to be the way we want it to be rather than accepting whatever God works, as well as His time for His works to come to fruition. Much of what has been written here has been learned through the mishaps and what people might think "should not be." There were definitely points during the midst of more significant impact from others' body pain (earlier in this walk of being present), that I questioned whether or not "watching and being in true identity" would really work in connection to that body pain. What I found, however, is that all body pain will continue to dissolve as we persevere and give it some time under the Lord's light. Becoming truly present is a gradual awakening.

While remembering to allow for God's work in His time, the importance of watching to remain present so that the old self doesn't dominate us is a discipline. Discipline leads to self-discipline. When children receive no discipline from the outside (from parents), they have not learned and are then unable to be self-disciplined. That is the case with children who have ADHD and ADD as a whole. With these children, newly initiated parental discipline can begin to train into their children self-discipline (although it takes a good bit to undo the old training). Similarly, people can gain self-control over the fleshly mind when it receives discipline from them so that it cannot dominate them constantly. In other words, when we say no to the old self's rampages about the future or the past and we do not allow it to run out of control, it loses power to run over us (like an ADHD child running over his or her parents). This requires practice to develop this discipline, and the Lord usually gives us plenty of opportunities when He works to cause us to walk further with Him. He who "practices the truth [and does not participate with darkness] comes to the light" (Jn. 3:19-21). This verse and those verses around it are about practicing the truth of the cross, of losing (by not participating with) the old life and its darkness so as to find true life and light. Losing or fasting the old self, especially its body pain, is about us saying no to its "doing what it wants." Also, when we do not participate with others' body pain, it receives discipline as well, and it helps them to have self-discipline in those areas. And when we undergo consequences connected to stepping in our own body pain, when we receive it as such, it begins to bring about greater self-discipline in us as well.

In summary regarding watching body pain and gaining self-discipline or self-control governed by the Spirit, the amount of self-control we have depends upon the amount of ground of the old self within us in a given area. When there is much old ground in a particular area, it is usually because we carry with us in our body significant emotional energy from previous impact. You can actually feel that emotion, anxiousness, and pain when a current situation ignites it again. When this kind of significant body pain becomes touched by a present situation, we usually have little to no self-control. We usually lose contact with the present moment in those situations, and we therefore lose contact with Presence and the fruits that accompany Presence. The simple test as to whether we are under the influence of body pain at the moment is whether or not we experience the fruits of the Spirit. When we don't experience the Lord's fruits, we are in the old self and its body pain. And as mentioned earlier, the only real ways to dissolve that pain are for us to do the following: 1) to fast or discontinue the ways that we walk that either feed that ground in us or that put ourselves in situations that keep that ground being heightened in us (which means not striving or doing anything from insecure, earthly energy at the moment, but pausing to disconnect from that energy), 2) to pay attention to joining with our unseen true identity that is not attached to anything of this world, and 3) to come back to the present as soon as we are able, either during the circumstance or immediately following it, to simply watch the sinful mind of man in us (the thoughts as well as the emotions that are simply reactions to the thinking that is running in us).

When regularly walking in the present and watching like that described above, we will find that the light of Presence continually causes the old self and its ways to lose power. We find that we gradually become more present, truly conscious, and spiritually awake. We become aware of what we do in life as opposed to being oblivious to the pain we cause when striking out because of being governed by the old self and its body pain. The earthly thoughts and emotions, while being watched with the light of the Lord's Presence, become exposed for the tares or "things" they are and they begin being burned away and transformed into light.

*Be still and watch, not participating with any earthly energy (waiting till it dissipates), especially during body pain and difficulties with significant others. Watch not outwardly in fear, but inwardly such that the mind of the old self within you does not overtake you like a thief and make you unconscious of what you do. You may even want to take space and reread this chapter at times of body pain being ignited. When hurt occurs because of body pain, from you or from another, may it be like Jesus said, "Forgive them, for THEY KNOW NOT WHAT THEY DO."*

*For those who are unaccepting of imperfection and sin, have no other focus than letting go of everything and simply agreeing with the Lord that you are acceptable and loved in your sinful areas with no striving needed. Let Him do the work, for He is faithful when we trust Him.*

# Watching and Not Judging: Starting with What You Do Have

"Then the kingdom of heaven will be comparable to ten virgins, who took their lamps, and went out to meet the bridegroom" (Matt. 25:1). The oil in the lamps of the wise virgins is about those who are present and "watch with the Spirit" for the Bridegroom. While all the virgins fell asleep (like all of us will do at points), the wise followers of the Lord, those with oil, will watch with the Spirit and will enjoy a wedding feast with the Lord each time He comes – for His coming is not in a single "day" or "time" as we know it. For one day is as a thousand years and a thousand years as one day – because He is always present but will come in a "way" or "time" we do not expect. Watching for some single day in some future time is actually what causes people to fall asleep. Rather, when we know His coming is always "at hand," we will remain more alert and watchful. Also, oil, the Spirit, cannot be given by us to another as seen in this parable. We can only watch with the oil directly given to us by the Lord. Nobody else can truly watch for us.

This kind of watching with the Spirit for the Bridegroom, however, is different than watching within regarding the old self and its tricks to cause us to leave the present. While this kind of watching is still watching with the Spirit so our eye is single, it is watching life to see *how* the Bridegroom comes to meet His bride. Your portion of Christ within is part of the bride that He is constantly gathering into One. When watching with the Spirit, we can see life from His perspective and what He is after in a given moment. When watching with the Spirit during difficult life situations, we are able to remain present and see that there is no true problem at the moment. We can feast with the Lord and with what His spiritual food is at the moment.

Watching without oil, without the Spirit, however, leaves us in a place of making judgments about what ought to be in life. Then, through the eyes of the old self, we will see plenty of times that life is not as we think it should be. Plenty of "problems" seem to arise. However, *any judgments and inner resistance about "what is" is the beginning of death.* Making our own judgments about life occurs when we have shoulds and expectations about what ought to be. When we make our own judgments about the moment that essentially resist "what is" (God's current provisions), we create negative emotions. We create problems in our mind that the mind then feels a need to work out somehow – which cannot be done because they are self-created problems. All of this occurs because of us making judgments about God's provisions (like Adam and Eve) rather than first accepting what is. When we make judgments, we become a victim regarding a situation. We shift to the old self, and as a victim, listen to the serpent again, just like back in the garden. We don't know God's love, mainly because we believe the enemy's lies that somehow God must not really be for us or have our best interest in mind.

Whatever is real cannot be hurt. Only shadows of the real can be hurt. When Adam and Eve originally sinned, God did not curse Adam, the true spirit-breathed person, but instead, cursed *the ground* that his flesh was made from (Gen. 3:17). In other words, the ground or dust that Adam's flesh was made from, and then was cursed, is the same as the flesh that is opposed to God that Paul in the New Testament said we are not to join with during our walk (see Rom. 7:23-24; 8:5-8). So there was never a curse toward the true, spirit person that God created but only toward the outer, separating fleshly person. That was what God's "wrath" in the Old Testament was always towards. Because the flesh, the false self, was opposed to God, that left us with a choice as to which part we would participate with – the fleshly, false self, or the true spirit person within. And God's sovereignly placed trials during life are what God has always used to strip us from the fleshly self so as to free our true self. What is true cannot be hurt but will all return and be joined in one spirit with the Lord in the end. Only the shadow, the fleshly earthly self can be hurt. And if our soul only joins with the fleshly self, we will experience the hurt and stripping because we will not be in the real or true self we were meant to walk in. Fortunately, God keeps working to strip us of the flesh self so as to free our true that has been hidden and imprisoned beneath the flesh. When we finally experience heaven more fully after leaving this earth, we will be surprised to find that we (the true self) were never really hurt nor could ever really be hurt. Only the fleshly, false self could be hurt.

So in a sense, there are no "problems" or issues in life except those we create when operating from the old self that makes its own separate judgments about life. We only create imaginary problems when we are in the separate, individualistic old self and want life different than it is. Yes, we do encounter difficult life situations, but not problems. A life situation is sovereignly made for us at the moment, first to honor, accept, and see accurately, and second, to either deal with, continue to accept as it is, or leave.

While wrongful, hurtful behavior by another to us is not ultimately how God wants something to remain (nor does it justify the behavior), it is sovereignly allowed by God for us to first accept at the moment *for* the purpose of sensing and learning how to step with Him in new ways *so as to be freed*. If from the old self we resist a situation or demand that it be different, we are not in a position to learn from God in that moment. Because we often repeat old steps in familiar, difficult situations, the primary way of new growth is God allowing another similar situation for us to learn a "new move" from Him in that area. But we can only learn from Him if we first honor and accept the moment as if it is supposed to be there. There are no problems or lapses in God's sovereignty. Problems only really exist in our mind when we do not accept and deal with life as it is.

When we accept and deal with life as it is rather than fearfully reacting in the old self, however, it is essentially about our flesh self swallowing life's trials and difficulties in a way that further frees the true self – just as this way of walking is symbolically illustrated in the book of Revelation (12:15-16), "Then from his mouth the serpent spewed water like a river, to overtake the woman [the body of Christ on earth] and sweep her away with the torrent. But the earth helped the woman by opening its mouth and swallowing the river, that the dragon had spewed out of his mouth." Let our own earth (our flesh) be like the scriptures say, accepting, receiving, and swallowing (allowing) the raging rivers of this world as they are, trials and all, even if they seem to be from the enemy – rather than us insisting that life be different than it is. This way of walking is, again, the way of the cross to lose the old life so as to bring more true life.

One more clarification about swallowing, allowing, or accepting life's trials is crucial, however. Initial acceptance is not about passively being a doormat. *Initial* acceptance or allowance of even a very wrongful action from another toward yourself is simply for providing initial space and freedom for the Lord to be able to reach and lead you. If we don't have that initial acceptance of the situation as it is, we invariably react according to the old self. Having that initial space, however, allows the Lord to be our eyes, and as a result, our wisdom – which may mean, for example, removing ourselves from that wrongful behavior of that other person.

At one point in my life, some wild teenagers drove by and shot a hole through the picture window in my house with a pellet gun. I could have resisted that moment saying that it shouldn't have happened, meanwhile leaving a hole in the window during the middle of winter. That is what we sometimes try to do by saying (from our old self) that life shouldn't happen how it does. Even though I didn't cause the hole in the picture window, I was still left with a life situation to deal with. That life situation would have only become a "problem" in my mind if I had resisted facing it as it was. That is what happens when we make judgments about life situations. We temporarily avoid dealing with life as it is. And yet, life situations, just like this one, are specifically designed to help us learn to let go of earthly life little by little so as to free and grow our true identity that is not of this world. Everything is for us, that is, for the true, spirit self.

When we make judgments about life, we treat ourselves like we are separate and not connected to life and what God made. That is the selfish, individualistic self that wants life how it wants it rather than peacefully relating with God and His sovereign works. Judging life also treats God like He is separate from us and all that He created, as if He is a separate Self like our separate, earthly self.

When we judge life, we begin from a position of "what we do not have." We start with a perceived deficit and place of lack, and then ultimately, insecurity and fear. Anytime we start from a perceived place of lack, it is a negative that births more negative. For example, fear begets fear, or like the scriptures say, "Bloodshed begets bloodshed." But anytime we judge life not to be as we think it should be, we begin with a perceived place of lack that, if anything, brings more lack in one form or another. This is, again, exactly what happened in the garden of Eden. Adam and Eve, listening to the serpent's lies, judged life as not in their best interest. Immediately after eating the forbidden fruit, then, they continued perceiving lack (nakedness) on their end. That was the beginning of people walking in the old self that creates problems in their minds. It was the beginning of walking under lies and blindness about believing we are in a place of lack and, therefore, need something different than God provides. It was the beginning of being afraid of God and walking in a way that demonstrates we do not know or trust Him and His love. It was also the beginning of always starting with what we do not have rather than what we do have. When we say, "Something is wrong" connected to current life circumstances, or even regarding how we are "not doing so well" in our Christian walk, we make judgments and start from a perceived place of lack rather than from a place of trust. In contrast, it is written in the scriptures (2 Cor. 8:12), "For if the readiness is present, it is acceptable according to what a man has, not according to what he does not have." While this verse was about "giving," this is still an overall spiritual principle established by God – it is acceptable what we do have.

What *do* you have? When Jesus walked the earth, He healed, restored, and redeemed through what He had, not from what He did not have. When the lame beggar looked to Peter and John for money, Peter exclaimed (Acts 3:6), "I do not possess silver and gold, but what I do have I give to you: In the name of Jesus Christ the Nazarene — walk!" What Peter had was Christ, His love, and healing power. Christ and all that He has comes from what we already have, not from what we do not have (he who has, more shall be given, but he who does not have, what he has shall be taken away – see Matt. 13:12).

Striving for what we do not have is one of the enemy's greatest deceptions. When we strive for anything that we do not currently have, it is all a lie, and it is the "taking" by the old self that does not know God – the very same taking we saw by Adam and Eve in the garden (and the tree of life and its fruits were guarded by a flaming sword such that taking could no longer gain true life). Striving and taking are from distrust and not truly knowing God and His love. God is I AM. He always IS. Anytime we consider the moment to be not as it is supposed to be, we treat God as if He ISN'T. Just like Adam and Eve back in the garden of Eden, we treat God like He and His present provisions are not up to our satisfaction. Whether it is hurtful or even horrendous actions on the part of another to us or whether it is an injury or accident, God always IS. The present moment is always His provisions for us. It's just that some of those "difficult" provisions are beyond our earthly understanding; and they are not even supposed to be "earthly good" at those times, but rather, good for producing heavenly freedom and fruits.

True life is not about this earth. True satisfaction cannot be obtained from impermanence. The earth and all it contains that the old self tells us we need can never bring true satisfaction because all created matter is impermanent; it is insecure because it will all be destroyed at some point. In contrast, Jesus said (Jn. 7:37-38), "If anyone is thirsty, let him come to Me and drink. Whoever believes in Me, as the Scripture has said, streams of living water will flow from within him." Only Living Water brings true life and satisfaction because He is ever living and ever present. And when we trust that He is always present and we remain present with Him, the scriptures say that streams of living water will flow from within us. That living water will flow from within us because He is the living water within us that we have trusted. At those times of trusting Him, we have joined in further establishing His true and everlasting satisfaction within us. We experience a little more fullness or completion that never leaves us. When we treat Life like it's not as it should be, however, we are not turned toward the Lord as our Shepherd and we will usually be in a place of want that seems unable to be satisfied (see Ps. 23:1).

The original taking of the apple is very symbolic of how the world trains and even rewards us for rising up and taking life for ourselves in some way. For the majority of people, their whole world is oriented towards a constant taking of the apple, but this time, it is the apple from the tree of life we try to take (and we will get cut at some point by the sword that guards that tree). For people as a whole, all thoughts, feelings, and actions are typically bent toward being competent and taking the apple of life. Then, the world encourages and applauds us when we have done well at taking the apple. It's almost as if doing well at taking the apple is the world's rite of passage for teens to become "competent" adults. The real problem, however, is that all that energy toward striving and taking builds a powerful fleshly, old self that is deeply unconscious and spiritually asleep. That foundation is one of sand and will gradually disintegrate during the Lord's storms of life. The powerful, separate earthly self is essentially a sandy foundation that requires the Lord bringing in a more powerful way of the cross so as to free us from that dominating old self. But the point is that striving to take the apple of life is still the continuance of one of the greatest deceptions by the enemy.

Wanting something more than "what is" in the moment is clear evidence of the energy of the old self. Each current moment is present for our learning, enduring, or a new step in life and when we resist it or want something different from the moment, we lose contact with the present moment and with Him who IS. As soon as we have any inner resistance to any given moment, we essentially say to the Lord that what we have is not what He should have done or allowed. But we can only join with the Lord to make more new life from what we presently have. You can see this spiritual principle in Jesus' feeding of the five thousand (Mk. 6:37-38), "But He answered and said to them, 'You give them something to eat!' And they said to Him, 'Shall we go and spend two hundred denarii on bread and give them something to eat?' And He said to them, 'How many loaves *do you have*? Go look!'" Can you see that the Lord tested them for a purpose? Can you see that the disciples immediately thought life was demanding something beyond what they had? And then they thought that they needed life or self to be different than "what was" in some way. Miracles, healing, restoration, and new life only come from what we presently have. That was the lesson from the feeding of the five thousand. Jesus "broke" the bread *that they did have*, and "gave thanks" (vs. 41) rather than being perturbed about what they did not have in their circumstances. In the end, there were still 12 basketfuls of broken bread left. The brokenness is about bread being broken or poured out from Himself. It is Him giving of Himself and giving all that He has and is – His present life being poured out for others. That is the way we are to walk as well, that we would give of what we presently have, not from what we don't have. Then, from being in union with Him, we will produce new life when we give of that life to others.

All of this giving of life, however, is about us giving from what we do have, not from what we don't have. This kind of giving points clearly to a way of walking that is not concerned at all about what we don't yet have. And anytime we are dissatisfied with the present moment and wish it to be different than it is, we essentially start with what we don't have in some way. It is folly; it is an illusion. Anytime others are dissatisfied with us at the moment, as if we need to be more than we are, it also is folly and illusion. The only way to bring further life, goodness, and heavenly riches is to start with what we do have – to start with "what is" and give thanks rather than to start with "what should be." Starting with "what is" starts with Who IS, and new life can always be formed from Who IS.

There is never security and life available when we believe the present moment is not as it should be. Only fear and death result. When the present moment is perceived as not good enough, it clearly indicates that we have projected our hope onto some different scenario we have envisioned, or really, imagined. That is misplaced hope, misplaced "salvation." When our hope is in something different than what is, our hope is not in God who IS. When we desire something to be different than it is at the present moment, even regarding ourselves, we neither honor what is nor the God who is the worker and perfecter of all things. We do not honor the moment, and, in essence, look for salvation in some future time or some alternative way than what God designed. Even when noticing our inadequacy, which is really the old self's inadequacy, we are not to "try to grow," because the impetus is from dissatisfaction about the earthly self (which is not who we are anyway). When we try to grow, that is the old self trying to "save ourselves" again. The Lord said not to save our lives but to lose them, for the more we try to save ourselves from inadequacy in whatever form, the more we feed the dissatisfaction of the old self and the growth eludes us. In fact, that kind of striving always feeds and further strengthens the old self.

All of our satisfaction, fulfillment, hopes, and projections that are placed onto the future, or at least onto something different than what is, are a wild goose chase that never ends. In those unending loops, we are caught in time and imagination, and it never saves us. Hope and salvation can only be in the present with the Lord who is I AM and can only come through honoring and accepting His present provisions (which includes accepting ourselves as we are). Satisfaction and fulfillment come through the present by abiding in the Lord. That is how He delivers us. When our hope is truly in Him and His present provisions as He IS, then we receive heavenly riches and true satisfaction from Him. He produces the growth, not us. He produces the growth by us simply being in agreement with Him, what He is working, and what His provisions are at the moment. Agreeing with Him means rest and peace. Anything else is futility. Anytime we have a perceived lack, it is staring at and participating with the old clothing and we have not clothed ourselves in Christ and His sufficiency that is in the present.

Paul wanted a thorn taken from him, so he entreated the Lord three times to remove the thorn. In other words, Paul wanted something different than "what was" at that point. He likely believed that whatever the "lack" was should not have been. The Lord responded, however, by saying (2 Cor. 12:9) "My grace is sufficient for you." In essence, the Lord conveyed, "My provisions and grace in the present moment are enough." When we are content with the present moment *as* God's provisions, we will find that His grace actually is sufficient. Also, the Lord's power in us is further built or strengthened when He leaves us in places of perceived lack – and we learn that we were not really in a place of lack after all. When we remain in the present, where God's grace is, there is never truly lack. We only perceive (and therefore experience) lack when the mind of the old self tells us that something or someone in the moment is not what should be. But Christ wants us to know, just like He said to Paul, that His grace is always sufficient for us – so let our hearts not be troubled by the lies of the false self about something lacking in the moment.

Granted, we can all attest to "experiencing" lack in life at certain moments – but it would also be true that we did not walk the way of the cross by abiding in Him in the present moment either. In other words, had we walked in the present moment being content with His provisions, His grace would have been present and therefore sufficient, and we would not have experienced true lack. The deception about lack has been our "problem" since Adam and Eve. We have been naked since then, not clothed in belief in the sufficiency of Christ. Our only real insufficiency the whole time has been our lack of belief in Him, His love, and His provisions when we judge life not to be as we think it should be. That has been our sin. That has been our nakedness. But as we walk in the way of the cross that our Master walked, simply in the present trusting in Him and His provisions, we become clothed and find that we were never really in lack or insufficiency – except for not believing Him. That is why it is simply belief and trust in Him that clothes us. "Behold, I am coming like a thief. Blessed is the one who stays awake and keeps his garments, lest he walk about naked and men see his shame" (Rev. 16:15). The Lord comes like a thief to take and cause lack regarding our old clothes and self so that we would be awakened and stay awake to keep our true clothes that were always within. Let us keep watch.

*Cease saving yourself; lose your earthly, separating "I". Cease striving to take because of distrust of God, and trust not in your own earthly perceptions of the challenges you encounter. Rather, accept and honor your circumstances and yourself as God has provided; rest and trust "what you do have" so as to remain present with He who is.*

# We Were Meant to Be Present:
## Seeing Its Power At a Practical Level

If you watch life to learn about being present, you will see ways that people demonstrate a deeper desire to be present, although it is covered up most of the time by the old self that tries to control life and save itself. Athletes and those who push the extreme and live life on the edge do so because they get in touch with the aliveness that they were meant to walk in. When the "extreme sports" athletes or risk-takers push the edge, they need to be very, very present, or the alternative would likely be serious injury or death. Also, to go to a "beyond human level," which was our destiny that these risk-takers are drawn to, they must be extremely present. When you watch great athletes, you will notice that all their focus is in the present moment, and when it is, the moment seems to move them to a level beyond normal athletes. If you have experienced those kinds of moments, you likely have sensed the richness and alertness to the depth of the usually unnoticed details of the moment. That is what being truly present does. We see, hear, and learn more than the normal person in life when we are truly present. The only problem is that the Lord wants us to learn to be present in our daily walk, not through risking in a way that constantly lives life on the edge.

Very romantic, intimate times of oneness with a person are

similar to what was described above. In fact, "one-withness," which will be described later, is most represented on this earth by godly, sexual union. A true one-withness in times of intimacy is more about truly being present with one another than the physical act of sexual union. True intimacy is when two people are truly present in a way that is one-with one another. In that kind of intimacy, there is a true noticing, honoring, and "seeing" of one another. The moment slows down such that the richness, quality, and Spirit of the moment become more than natural life. The goal is not physical union but being one-with one another in a way that is truly present and honoring of one another as well as the moment. At those times, each person experiences a richness and quality of life that is not normally experienced in "regular life." Each person interacts with the other person in a way that conveys that nothing is more important than valuing the other person at the moment. And yet, this kind of richness and quality of life is the way life was meant to be between people as a whole, as opposed to barely noticing one another during the typical daily routines of life.

That same kind of richness and quality of life is also true in times of intimacy, stillness, and oneness with the Lord – as long as we remain in the present moment with Him. I had been drawn to contemplation and meditating on the scriptures for quite a while before learning that it was all about being present. For many years I had meditated on the scriptures, sometimes being present and sometimes working at it in the old mind. And for the last few years, I had been becoming more still, being drawn to contemplation as a whole. However, my times of contemplation were unexplainably fruitful or not fruitful. Only after learning more fully about being present had those areas become regularly fruitful – because without being present at earlier points, the fruits and the grace were not really available. Often during those earlier times of stillness, my mind would usually run and work at future things. Upon learning about being present, however, I noticed that the richness, rest, peace, and the Lord's perspectives were generally available (unless the Lord was pouring me out like I mentioned previously).

Whenever situations from the past arise where we remember the many details so vividly, that is evidence of situations where we were very present. Consider some of those memories. Can you see the difference of the depth of detail, richness, and learning that occurs when we are very present versus when we are not? Those who hunt or fish often tell the stories of their great catch in vivid detail even years after it had occurred. That is because they were extremely present when the event occurred and, as such, they can describe the situation as if it had just occurred yesterday. The opposite is also true. Shortly after learning about the significance of being present in life, I experienced the absence of the above kind of richness and learning because of not being present in a particular situation. One morning I parked in the huge parking lot like I typically do for my job. I parked wherever I found a space because there was no assigned parking. I knew I would shortly be facilitating a significant meeting regarding a colleague who was in a place of serious difficulty, and my mind was working much about what all was to come. Meanwhile, I had taken about ten steps from my car toward the building, and awareness came upon me about being present again. As I became present, God got my attention and I turned back and looked at my car. I became overwhelmed at the spiritual principle that God was now revealing to me: I realized that I would have had no clue regarding the whereabouts of my car at the end of the day. I saw that little to no learning occurred when my mind was not fully present in the moment. *Whether my mind would have been on the past or about the future, learning would not have been able to take hold well because of me not being in the present moment.*

Another situation that taught me much about the contrast of rushing towards the future versus being in the present (as well as about the difference in power between the two) was regarding the many emails that I receive daily at work. I had been learning about not being resistant to the moment and, instead, trying to honor each moment. The next morning at work, I opened up the emails and saw nearly 80 emails. I sighed with irritation about all of the emails that I needed to respond to. Immediately, I caught my sigh and resistance to the moment. I realized that it was normal for me to sigh about the many emails. As I watched what the old self and its thinking within me was trying to tell me, I saw the "good, logical rationale" – and yet, I saw that it was the old self. The old self tried to convince me, "I am made to be with people and to make a difference in people's lives, not to waste my time handling unending menial administrative tasks." But as I watched, I saw that it was a necessary part of my job and that resisting the emails only made me exhausted and sometimes miserable by the end of each day. By the time I got to the people part of my job, I was so worn out that I wasn't as effective as I could have been at that point anyway. So I decided to honor each email as if it was my only email. Once I got through that one, then I would do the same with the next one. No hurrying or forward-slanted moment whatsoever. As I regularly honored each moment (and email) in that way more and more, I found that I experienced the fruits of the Spirit so much more fully and regularly – even dealing with all the emails. From the best I can tell, I got more done because I was less exhausted in the long run. I also realized that I cared much better for people through the emails as well as when I got to the more interactive people aspect of my job. I saw more fully the power of being present and the spiritual fruits that accompanied being present.

Another way you will see the power of what being present does is through true emergencies. If you have ever been in a true emergency or have talked in detail with someone who has, you will find that life occurs in slow motion (depending upon how much of an emergency exists). I have experienced this several times in my own life. I have also talked with someone who had experienced this "slow motion" when his lower leg was taken off in a warehouse accident. The Lord provides extra grace during true emergencies to help us slow down so that we become extremely present. That is what happened with this man. Standing beside the bucket loader, he reached in to the seat to grab something while accidentally bumping it into reverse. It began backing up with the bucket tight against the concrete floor, catching his foot first and then taking off his lower leg in front of his eyes. While visiting him in the hospital, I had commented about how extremely painful that must have been. He said, "That's the funny thing. I never experienced any pain; it's as if my leg was numb. Everything went to slow motion while I was watching every detail at the moment as if it wasn't me" (because, really, it was only the earthly him that he was watching). To me, I would say that the Lord provided extra grace to slow him down to be very present, and being present, he was very joined to his true indestructible identity within. That is who was watching and why he didn't really experience any pain during the accident. He was the true self that couldn't be hurt. He was not the outer shell of flesh going through some horrible earthly experience, but rather, was the true identity that was partaking of the divine at that moment. This incident, to me, seemed to remind me of how Stephen being stoned was more in touch with the Lord's presence at the moment than with what was happening to him earthly-wise. Stephen was abiding in his true, rather than earthly, identity. Are you getting a sense of "His ways that are higher than our ways of the earth" that become available as we learn to participate more in our true identity rather than our earthly one?

We have all heard of or encountered people who have been in true emergencies and the extraordinary things that seem to occur at those times. We're all aware of stories of an ordinary person lifting with his or her bare hands a tractor or car when it had fallen on someone they loved, or, of someone diving in front of an oncoming car to push someone out of the way, fully knowing that they would be killed. These are examples of a force or power deeper within that is greater than the outer shell that we have thought to be ourselves. While extraordinary feats have often been explained away as adrenaline, what produces that adrenaline? It is the power of the portion of Christ placed within, and it is a power beyond this world.

When we imagine being in other people's horrible earthly situations that are beyond what we believe "should" happen in life, we are told "Don't get ahead of God." In other words, there is a grace in horrible situations that sustains people, and we have none when we simply imagine being in those situations. That is the same thing that happens when we "dwell" in the future or the past. But for people who are in true emergencies, there is a slowing down and being fully present. All your attention is powerfully drawn to the present for there is no time to think of the future or past. When something horrible is presently happening in life, your mind does not have the luxury (or, really, problem) of thinking of the many other things it usually thinks of. These kinds of situations really illustrate the difference of what being present does and the miraculous grace that comes with being truly present.

If we watch life with wisdom, we will see that we were always meant to be present, and therefore in true relationship with God and with others. We can see that, by being truly present, there is a richness and aliveness that cannot be found any other way. That is why Jesus said that if we wanted to be His disciples, we would need to walk the way of the cross, the way He walked in the present that cared not about saving the earthly life and self. Walking in the present like that was the way of richness, aliveness, and love. It was what we were meant for; it is our heavenly home in Him. Let us ask the Lord for this gift that we would dwell there. The psalmist said (Ps. 65:4), "How blessed is the one whom Thou dost choose, and bring near to Thee, to dwell in Thy courts. *We will be satisfied with the goodness* of Thy house, Thy holy temple."

*Be still and be awakened to what the power of being present really does.*

# If the Eye is Clear, the Whole Body is Filled with Light: Watching in Other Ways

Watching produces more light. We can watch in the present moment in union with the Lord in various ways. In union with Him, we can watch and meditate on His truths in life, and let Him teach us. For example, we might pay attention to the impermanence of all created things and become aware of how "no thing" is really nothing that can bring true satisfaction to us. We can watch through the Lord's eyes, and as such, "see through" the unending striving that the world convinces us is needed for finding true life. We can also join with the Lord and watch whatever we do in the moment as a simple means of staying grounded in the present. We might watch or notice our actions, our thinking, our emotions, or even our breathing. Noticing our breathing and realizing that it is His spirit-breathed life that is in us is a great way to become grounded in Him again, as well as to disrupt the dominant thinking of the mind of the old self.

For people that are not expressive and not very attuned to their inner experiences and, thus, not present or awake regarding their current state (as to whether they are in their true identity or in the old self), an "I am aware" exercise is a great way to become more present. This exercise is to continue completing the sentence "I am aware …" with very simple experiences that you become aware of during the day. Begin with first recognizing that the Lord desires to be with you and to help you become more awakened to each present moment, and second, continue completing "I am aware" statements while noticing or watching in union with the Lord. For instance, I am aware of a little ache in my foot. I am aware of feeling hungry. I am aware of feeling a little empty and alone, and so on. You can do this exercise for as little or as long as you wish for learning to become awakened to your experiences in each present moment (so that the old self is less likely to overtake you).

Watching in the present moment in union with the Lord lifts us to a higher level spiritually because we become filled with light the more we watch in union with Him. Being filled with light and lifted to a higher level spiritually is becoming grounded in Mount Zion. Mount Zion is "beautiful in elevation" (Ps. 48:2), above the things of the world. When we have somewhat longer periods of being present, especially through watching life with the Lord's eyes, we begin to flood ourselves with the light of His presence. Our whole body becomes filled with light when the eye is clear or single, and we are lifted to a higher elevation than the things and ways of the world. Many people have experienced this being lifted to a higher spiritual level when their eye was single or clear during times of praise and worship. When we are "lost" in praise and worship, that is simply another form of meditation and single-mindedness on the Lord and His perspectives. That is the same experience that happens through a peaceful, more pure watching that simply notices the present moment from His eye deeper within us. We are lifted to a higher spiritual level where we are filled with light and more aware of the things of God.

This brighter light and higher spiritual wave-length creates greater protection from the darkness and lower spiritual wavelengths. Like attracts like. In essence, we become less susceptible to darker forces and more in tune with the Lord and His forces of light the more we have filled our body with the light of His presence through simply watching with Him. Just like how we can reinforce or strengthen the old self and its lies by further joining with those lies, we can reinforce and strengthen the new identity and the respective fruits every time we are present, even if that is brief at points. In essence, we can accumulate more of the Lord's presence and His fruits the more we become present even if it is little by little. I have experienced the difference of not being present for most of a day and the anxiety and lack of peace that become built up through that kind of day, as well as more of the fruits of the Spirit and peace when I had even some moments of being present during a day. Some of being present very much helps versus none.

Do we actually believe the scriptures? The Lord said our whole body is *filled* with light if our eye is clear or single. As I mentioned above, we have literally experienced this higher place or filling of light during times of praise and worship. That experience is the scriptures coming true. Our true body of light is further filled with light when our eye is single or clear during some kind of watching in union with the Spirit. This true body of light is the body we will retain when we physically die, for the scriptures say "May your spirit and soul *and body* be preserved complete" (1 Thess. 5:23). The body of flesh will not be retained, but our spiritual body of light beneath the fleshly outer garment will be retained. That is our true body and our true identity in Christ that is placed within us. We just haven't as yet truly identified with that identity, or put that garment on (because of identifying more with the earthly physical things that can be seen). And yet, *the real is the unseen*, not the seen. What is seen is only a shadow of what is real.

Even what is seen was made from that which was unseen, for the scriptures say (Heb. 11:3), "By faith we understand that the worlds [the universe] were prepared by the word of God, so that what is seen was not made out of things which are visible." This makes more evident that the real is the unseen that made and became all that we see as well. The formless became form, and yet the real is the formless and unseen that we are to pay attention to. That is how the scriptures continually exhort us. We are to keep our minds on heavenly things, the unseen things above (higher in spiritual elevation) rather than temporal things. Being "hidden with Christ" is when we abide in our true identity within that is in Him, for the scriptures say (Col. 3:3), "For you have died and your life is hidden with Christ in God."

One way to watch the unseen, beyond the watching at our gates regarding what occurs within us, is to "watch," sense, or experience the light that is within us. When we relax and simply pay attention to our true body of light just beneath the physical garment, we can sense a radiant energy. That is our true body of light that is one with Christ. The more you pay attention to the unseen in this way, the more you can sense and join with the radiant energy of the light of Christ that is within. And the more you join with that light of Christ within, the more that true light is strengthened and becomes our frame of reference. Even now, pause, and pay attention to the pulsating energy you can feel in your body, hands, and legs. Give that experience some time and awareness. The more you get in touch with this light of Christ within, the more you can sense the strength of Christ that is our true identity. We have simply, as yet, joined very little with our true identity in Christ. The more you join with this true identity within, however, the more you will recognize the truth that we only become hurt when we are not joined with this true identity. When we abide in the true that is not tied to earthly definitions of self, "hurtful" earthly words and actions do not pertain at all to us. When we abide in the light of Christ within, we are free from those definitions of self that typically cause pain – because those definitions are only about the earthly, old self that is not us.

This way of watching or sensing regarding the true light within is, to me, one of the best ways for being in my true identity with Christ, as opposed to being in the earthly seeable identity. Just like you can make it a habit of watching at the gates, you can also make it your habit to pay attention to your true body of light within that is one-with Christ (but, again, do not strive from unrest in any way; only step in this way as the Lord inclines you). Likewise, every time you encounter the struggle of feeling the pressure to live up to some earthly identity (especially when needing to supposedly fulfill certain roles for significant others), you can make it a habit of yielding to being in your true body of light that is one-with Christ. And if that feels beyond reach in your present situation, then simply ask for greater grace in future situations to join and become one-with the light of Christ within you. Yielding to and joining with your true identity that is one-with the light of Christ within, as opposed to the earthly identity and roles, gradually continues to "kill" the old self and resurrect new life as well as your unseen identity within.

Jesus told us the Spirit is like the wind. The Spirit cannot be seen, but we can tell what He is doing by the movement of all that He touches. Just as we see the trees and flowers of the field freely bending to the way He is moving through the wind, we can see the need for us to bend freely with how God works His Spirit to move the things of life. That is paying attention to the moving of the unseen; it is keeping our minds on the things above rather than on the seen objects of the earth.

In contrast to the trees, flowers, and nature as a whole, however, we as a people tend not to bend so freely to the movement of the Spirit. Have you noticed the difference of what your experience is like when you watch nature versus the rest of the world? For me, I'm much more at peace and rest when watching nature. This secure, peaceful experience connected to watching nature is one step closer to the likeness and nature of the Spirit because there is no will that opposes God in nature. The trees and flowers simply bend with His wind, even to the point of breaking from strong winds if that is His will. With humans, our wills constantly resist the Lord's will in one form or another. There is automatically unrest, insecurity, and sometimes agitation or anger with us when we resist His will and sovereign movement. We come out of peace immediately at those times.

Another step closer to the full fruits and likeness of the Spirit is when we watch what is truly unseen. Because the Spirit is unseen and formless, our minds identify more with Spirit when we pay attention to that which is unseen and formless. Look around the room where you are sitting for a moment. Rather than looking at any of the objects or forms of created matter, watch the space or air in the room. Do this for several minutes while also paying attention to what you feel like.

Do you sense the relaxed sensation that comes over you? It is because you are keeping your mind on heavenly things, the things unseen rather than earthly things. When you pay attention to that which is unseen and formless just as the Spirit is, you identify more with the Spirit and the unseen (our true home) than the seen. Who are we? We are unseen spirits and are simply aliens in a foreign world of form and that which is seen. We do not truly belong here in the world of form, but in heaven, which is not as much about a geographical location as it is about a heavenly position or way. When we come to know heaven more fully, whether that is on this earth or after we physically die, we will see that heaven is not a thing but is, instead, about all being connected spiritually as one – connected with God and one another where we will be compelled by love to serve Him and one another.

What causes the difference in sensation and experience within us when we pay attention to the unseen? All created matter and that which has form will one day come to destruction, and is therefore, unstable and insecure. When we identify with form and the seen more than with the unseen, we will constantly experience more instability and insecurity. When we identify with the formless and unseen, however, we experience more of the stability and security of that which is beyond created and corruptible matter. Can you hear the difference of fruits that occur in connection to what we are more identified with? The more we identify with the unseen and our true identity that is one-with the Lord, the more we experience the fruits of the Spirit (and vice versa). That is why it is good practice to pay attention to all the unseen – that is, notice the unseen spiritual happenings at the gates within us, our true body of light and energy within, the space or air in the room we are in, the unseen wind that causes trees and grass to bend and bow, or the silence that sounds are birthed out of. "God has chosen, the things that are not, that He might nullify the things that are" (1 Cor. 1:28). The overcomers referred to in the scriptures are those who overcome the created world of form. They are no longer a separate self, being at odds with a world of separate people and things. Rather, they are one-with the Lord, with His unseen sovereign works in the world, and with all that He loves. The world is no longer what holds their focus because they have identified more with Spirit and the unseen than with form.

How important is it to be in the now with what the Spirit works? How important is it that we work with Him and His wind that moves life the way He moves it rather than resisting life and He who works all things? There is a set of lengthy scriptures below that makes the importance of this kind of walk so utterly clear. In 2 Corinthians (6:1-10) it is written, "And working together with Him, we also urge you *not to receive the grace of God in vain* — for He says, 'At the acceptable time I listened to you, and on the day of salvation I helped you'; behold, *now* is 'the acceptable time,' behold, *now* is 'the day of salvation' — giving no cause for offense in anything, in order that the ministry be not discredited, but in everything commending ourselves as servants of God, in much endurance, in afflictions, in hardships, in distresses, in beatings, in imprisonments, in tumults, in labors, in sleeplessness, in hunger, in purity, in knowledge, in patience, in kindness, in the Holy Spirit, in genuine love, in the word of truth, in the power of God; by the weapons of righteousness for the right hand and the left, by glory and dishonor, by evil report and good report; regarded as deceivers and yet true; as unknown yet well-known, as dying yet behold, we live; as punished yet not put to death, as sorrowful yet always rejoicing, as poor yet making many rich, as having nothing *yet possessing all things.*"

Wow. That makes the importance of being in the present moment very clear – and the importance of not resisting whatever work the Lord is doing in the present moment, regardless of how difficult the work is. Those verses provide a hefty list of earthly difficulties. And yet, it is clear from Paul that the Lord works in and through all of those difficulties, and that we are to work together with Him during those difficulties rather than resist Him. That is where the grace is. We are to participate with how He as the wind moves in our life circumstances in each present moment. We are not only to see those difficult earthly circumstances as a time to serve Him but as a time of salvation (from the earthly) for us. Paul clearly emphasizes that salvation comes through the now, through the present circumstances even when they are difficult. That is where the grace is, a grace that we are not to receive in vain. And when we participate with Him in these ways, we "have nothing yet possess all things." When we are more identified with the unseen and His Spirit who moves like the wind, we will not identify with or desire to possess earthly form that is corruptible. In our minds controlled by the Spirit, we will neither care for nor be attached to (possess) those things; and yet, when we join with Spirit in moving heavenly mountains, those earthly things bow such that we end up possessing them after all.

When we do not participate with what is, even when that means difficulties or trials, we miss open doors or windows that were specifically designed for us. Any resistance to the present moment or any desire for life to be different than it is at the moment blinds us from the spiritual windows of opportunity that are present. When we cooperate with the unseen wind of the Spirit during life circumstances, however, abundant grace is always available for learning and growing in our true identity that is one-with Christ.

*Be still; set your minds on the unseen things of the Spirit. Notice your true body being filled with His light and energy as you become single-focused on the unseen.*

# Presence is Love:
## Honor the Moment
## through One-Withness

"Greater love has no one than this, that one lay down his life for his friends" (Jn. 15:13). Presence is this kind of sacrificial love. This is what God through Christ did and always does for us. When we are present we are then in a position to recognize the Lord's presence, which is a one-with kind of love as well as all His other fruits of the Spirit. But the greatest of the fruits and gifts to us is love.

Trying to love does not bring God's presence or His love to this earth. Love does not come from any earthly power of ours. At various times in life, we will find that we cannot simply make ourselves know love or express love well. That is because love is a gift that is not in our control. And yet, love is received, expressed, and given abundantly when we follow the way Christ walked before us. That is, when we walk the way of the cross that loses the old life such that we are simply in the present moment with Him, love is a given. Love comes *through* being present, for *being truly present is sacrificial just as love is sacrificial.* When we are sacrificially present, not trying to save our lives but one-with life just as Christ was, we pass out of death and into true life. In 1 John (3:14) the scriptures state, "We know that we have passed out of death into life, because we love the brethren. He who does not love abides in death." In other words, love is a result and the proof of walking in the present with true life, rather than saving our lives and walking in the past or future (which is death). Walking in death occurs when we try to save ourselves by controlling life as best as we can for the earthly security and glory of the old self. That is neither true life nor love. When we walk in the present in a way that loses the old life and its self-preservation, however, we walk with the richness of true life, and love will automatically be evident as John indicated.

As seen through Christ and His cross, His love is a sacrificial love that is one-with the object of His love. Nothing is held back. There is no self-preservation or self-protection in this kind of love. Even the verse about Him who knew no sin becoming sin on our behalf is exactly about Him being one-with the object of His love. This is a love that is the "greater love that lays down its life for all" because it sees all as its friend. When this love sees all as its friend, however, it sees the true identity we were meant to be, not the outer, old self that is the false identity. This love, then, works powerfully and unfailingly to free and love our true self inside, even at the cost of us losing our outer, false self since it is opposed to the true. When Love loves, it sacrifices its spiritually high position and becomes one with the object of its love such that it girds up, frees, and becomes one-with what it embraces. Then as that Love draws all into itself, the object of Love becomes transformed into the likeness of Love as well.

We see that Jesus loved us like that, and that He said when He walked this earth that He came to seek that which was lost. That is still His way that reaches out to us and embraces us in the lost places. That is what the truth of the gospel is all about. He is God who reaches out to be with us and save us with a one-with love when we allow Him to do so. There are various ways that we see evidence of a one-with kind of love on this earth that essentially reveal Him and His essence that are beyond this earth.

In terms of loving people, one who goes into the slums to live and be one-with those being loved is an example of this spiritual principle – in contrast to giving money from a distance. The Spirit, through such a person being in close godly relationship with those being loved, reaches and touches them. Also, effective, godly counselors become one-with the depths of their client's world such that the Spirit then moves them, providing support and direction from within that world rather than being apart from it.

While paling in comparison and yet giving just a glimpse of the Lord's one-with kind of love, when you closely watch exceptional artists, musicians, or athletes you can see *how* they perform beyond the normal ways of this earth. I remember watching a violinist that was well beyond the other, exceptional violinists. This violinist played while an orchestra with exceptional musicians accompanied his performance. I watched the faces of the musicians in the orchestra as they heard the violinist's beyond-human runs on his violin. These exceptional musicians in their own right sat in disbelief as this virtuoso performed seemingly impossible feats on his violin. When I watched this virtuoso, I could see that he was not in this world or realm. He was present to the utmost with his violin; he was one-with his violin. There was no separation.

Similarly, at another performance I saw an exceptional pianist that made the most distorted faces I had ever seen. He could have cared less about what the audience or anyone else thought of the many distorted faces he made – because he was not focused at all on this world. He had entered a world where he was one-with his piano and then played, as well, like he was not of this world. With great athletes, too, I have noticed that they "lose this world" and become one-with the experience of the moment regarding what they perform. They enter the "zone," or really, another realm of one-withness that allows the heavenly to work through them. Research on brain waves bears this out – that gifted persons in a profession become one-with the moment of the experience whereas novices focus primarily on the mechanics or skills of the profession. Gifted artists, as another example, are not concerned about the mechanics of how they paint but are one-with the experience of the moment as they paint. They become so present and absorbed into the experience of the moment that the world fades away. The world, then, is no longer their limit because another realm without earthly rules and parameters moves them. That realm is the realm of Spirit where there are no earthly boxes or procedures but simple freedom to be and express as the Spirit moves.

In the same way, spiritual disciplines become powerful through learning to lose this world and becoming one-with the experience of the moment. Meditating on the scriptures is losing this world and becoming one-with the scriptures such that the Spirit is free to move more fully about the scriptures. Prayer is not so much about asking for what we want or what we think ought to be but about becoming one-with the Lord and what He is presently working. Contemplation, as well, is not just about being still but about being fully present and one-with the Lord so as to see from His perspectives. Being one-with is Love manifested. When we move into the realm of one-withness we move into a place where a sacrificial love manifests itself, and because it cares not for itself, it is free. That is when True Creativity moves through us. That is walking in the power of Love. Spirit is freed and released when we lose this life and move into a one-with kind of love where we no longer save or control self. Because we no longer move or control ourselves, the Spirit is who moves us and we go beyond the limits of the earth. As the Lord continues to grow His people as a whole into loving with this kind of one-with love, we will see the works of heaven in ways of healing, miracles, and redemption like we've never seen before. Through being utterly present and one-with whatever we are to attend to at the moment, the Spirit can work and perform beyond what we ask for.

Becoming aware of when we have inner resistance to certain situations we encounter is crucial for being able to walk regularly in the power of love through one-withness. *Inner resistance is essentially the opposite of a one-withness where the Spirit performs great things.* The power and freedom of love is lost through resistance to the moment. In fact, inner resistance to "what is" in life is most often what takes us out of the present and into the past or future. Resistance and unacceptance of the present moment always strengthen the old self and its separate identity from Spirit. Paying attention to whether or not we resist the moment in life is one of the most important ways we can pay attention so as to stay awake and be present in life. If we resist, we "fall asleep" and cannot receive the Lord's goodness. Essentially, we "close our eyes, lest we see," as it says in the scriptures. When we encounter life difficulties, will we close our eyes, resist life, and become more asleep? Or, upon encountering difficulties, will we use those times to let go and accept rather than resist – to use difficulties to become more intensely awake and alert by watching in the Spirit? The more powerfully challenging or difficult a situation is, the more ongoing acceptance with being present is required. Death or deep loss in situations, for example, requires sustained "being one-with the loss and grief" while being present and accepting of the loss.

As a whole, resistance and negativity mean losing presence, whereas honoring the moment with a one-withness means increased presence as well as the fruits of the Spirit. Any unhappiness, negativity, or resistance regarding the moment means loss of the present and the fruits of the Spirit. This resistance may happen subtly or blatantly, but resistance automatically means unnecessary suffering. If you are currently suffering, usually it means that you are in the old self resisting life as it is, even if you are unaware that this subtle transition has taken place.

If you want significant growth in your walk with the Lord, watch the area of inner resistance. How often do you walk with subtle discontentment or resistance to the things you encounter in life? And yet, Jesus embraced with this one-withness all that He encountered. He first accepted and embraced whatever situation was at hand, and that is what allowed the Spirit of the Father in Him to move as the Father wished. There was always freedom within Jesus' heart that allowed the Spirit to have the freedom to move beyond the ways of the earth. But that freedom for the Spirit occurred because of Jesus first embracing with a one-withness whatever situation He encountered as if He had chosen it. The world would have called many of the situations that Jesus encountered "bad," and yet, Jesus embraced each of them with a one-with sacrificial love.

Love is able to be one-with because it sees no separation. Love does not judge and separate but joins and embraces. Whereas the old self judges, competes, compares, and desires a glorious, separate identity, the new self in Christ sees no separation because love is one-with all. "God has allotted to each a measure of faith. For just as we have many members in one body and all the members do not have the same function, so we, who are many, are one body in Christ, and individually members one of another" (Rom. 12:3-5). There is no separation. Earthly-wise, it only looks like there is separation. But it is only an illusion. "Now may the God who gives perseverance and encouragement grant you to be of the same mind with one another according to Christ Jesus; that with one accord you may with one voice glorify the God and Father of our Lord Jesus Christ" (Rom. 15:5-6). This passage is not about us trying to make each other be in agreement with one another. Rather, it is about not being in the individualistic, separating mind (the old self) but in the mind controlled by the Spirit. The mind controlled by the Spirit lets go of outcomes and perceived "necessary agreements" (which would be a contrived unity anyway). The mind of the Spirit is about love and allows the differing perspectives and gifts even if they are different from what we consider to be the right perspectives. With the mind of the Spirit, there is no lack because He will gather all unto Him in His time. The mind of the Spirit trusts Christ as the gap filler to *be* the unity amidst the differing perspectives and members of one spiritual body, which is one Spirit. That is One voice in the freedom of the Spirit; that is true unity. Likewise, that is the various branches being expressed by the single Vine when we no longer see our separateness but the oneness.

The Vine and the branches are not two (let alone many)

substances but one. They are not of two spirits but of One Spirit. While the branches can do nothing heavenly without the Spirit of the Vine, there is still One Spirit in all. There is no separation; Love is one-with. "And the glory which Thou hast given Me I have given to them; *that they may be one, just as We are one*; I in them, and Thou in Me, that they may be perfected in unity, that the world may know that Thou didst send Me, and didst love them, even as Thou didst love Me" (Jn. 17:22-23). "Even as Thou didst love Me." Wow. That is powerful. The Father loves us even as He loved Jesus, and His desire is that we become one even as Jesus and the Father are one. This is one-with.

The Father and Jesus are one, and we are to know and walk in that same kind of oneness. No separation. We see this lack of separation demonstrated in Acts (4:32), "And the congregation of those who believed were of one heart and soul; and not one of them claimed that anything belonging to him was his own; but all things were common property to them." This was the Spirit working a love that is one-with. When we love people with a one-withness, just like the one-withness demonstrated in exceptional violinists, artists, and athletes in their professions, we will experience the Spirit working with a freedom and power beyond the earth's limits. When we love with a sacrificial one-with kind of love, the control, human effort, and separateness begin to fall away such that the wind of the Spirit gives birth to the heavenly realm in more fullness.

Jesus never separated or made distinctions regarding others, and this was so evident that even the Pharisees saw this about Him. They said, trying to trap Jesus so as to accuse Him (Matt. 22:16), "Teacher, we know you are a man of integrity and that you teach the way of God in accordance with the truth. You aren't swayed by men, because you pay no attention to who they are." It is so clear here that Jesus paid absolutely no attention to people's earthly identity. He didn't separate whatsoever based upon earthly identity but saw all as children of God. Jesus' eye of no-separation between people, as well as between Himself and others, is part of what allowed Him to love all equally with a one-with kind of love. The Pharisees, however, didn't get to *experience* Jesus' love that way simply because they did not receive Him.

Perfect love casts out fear … in those who receive the Lord and His one-with love. There is no fear in love. Love is the most powerful force there is – because God is love. When love seeks that which is lost, meaning the dark places that do not know light or love, it seeks to join and become one-with those dark places such that they come to know love. When Love resides there being one-with that dark place, darkness can no longer withstand the power of light and love, but becomes dissolved into light and love. The darker, earthly elements melt before the power of love. That place that has not known light or love comes to know love, and the lies become seen for what they were. They hold no power anymore. And when there is no darkness or lies, there is no deception, and thus, no fear.

Perfect love casts out fear. Love conquers all in the end. That is why it is good for us to be very present and watchful with the eye of Spirit regarding whatever is not of light and love. When we persist in watching with the single eye of Spirit, all that is dark will bow under the power of light and love that casts out all that is not love. While this will not happen all at once because we will be unable to go immediately from not being present to constantly being present, participating this way will gradually conquer all that is not of God. Gradually, unwanted thoughts, emotions, body pain, and even traumatized body pain will dissolve. Likewise, unwanted earthly habits, sickness, diseases, and physical symptoms as a whole can dissolve and lose power through simply watching those darkened areas under the eye of Spirit, the eye of Love that casts out all fear and darkness. God wants to join with us as Love in the lost places. We have as yet, however, begun to know how to really believe and join with Him such that we experience His words coming true in full. That is what He is after, however – the knowing of Him and His secure love that fills the whole earth (Isa. 11:8-9): "And the nursing child will play by the hole of the cobra, and the weaned child will put his hand on the viper's den. They will not hurt or destroy in all My holy mountain, for the earth will be full of the knowledge of the Lord as the waters cover the sea." All will be brought under the power and security of Love in the end.

God is after people learning to keep watch so as to abide in the present with Him as a whole in life and to become present with a one-with kind of love in all that He sovereignly works. When "issues" do become present, we are no longer to separate and judge as if we are not one because there is only ever one issue: *are we present or not? Are we resisting life as it is that causes us to lose the present moment with Him?* Watching so as to be present takes care of everything because, upon truly being present with a one-withness, we will see that there are no separations and difficulties. When we are present in this way, we will see that the Lord's fruits are always available. And not being present always creates issues and problems. So let us watch like the five virgins who had oil in their lamps. Let us watch with the oil of the Spirit through the lamp of our body, the eye.

*Be still; see the world through the loving eyes of one-withness rather than separateness. Perfect love protects not itself but loves with a sacrificial love that casts out all fear.*

# Beware of the Leaven of the Pharisees: Hindrances to Presence

"For no man can lay a foundation other than the one which is laid, which is Jesus Christ" (1 Cor. 3:11). We have all tried at times in our lives to build from other foundations than from Christ alone. It all gets burned up when it is not of Christ. Only that which comes from Christ, His Spirit, and therefore His authority is His foundation and works. All that is not moved by Christ is not through His authority. That is why we can do good deeds that we believe God would want, and yet, when those deeds are moved by other motives (such as pleasing people or desiring self-glory), they don't produce truly good fruits. When something other than God and His love moves us, typically the works and the fruits will not be of God. And when the foundation is not of Christ, it is from the leaven or rules of the Pharisees. When people's motivation comes from an earthly teaching, system, way, or foundation rather than from a heavenly one, that is the leaven of the Pharisees. It is the leaven of the world. These fruitless works are motivated by the leaven or expectations of the world's systems and pleasing its leaders rather than from the authority of the Lord alone. Whether the expectations or rules are earthly rules or "spiritual" ones, when we are moved by rules and pleasing people who set the rules rather than being moved by the Lord Himself, we are moved by the leaven of the Pharisees.

One main way that we tend to be moved by something other than God is through the people systems we are part of. Virtually all people systems in one way or another "love" those who do what is expected and punish (even if subtly) those who do not conform. Within any people system, whether it is a family, community, school system, business, culture, or religious or spiritual system, people experience the rules, expectations, and rewards that are part of that system. From one group system to the next, it can become like high school clicks: "In this group we do it this way, not like that other group." Love is not experienced from a group when one does not belong to it. Even within a group, however, there is the pressure to conform to the rules and expectations of the group. If we stay within the group's expectations and rules, even if unspoken, we gain their rewards and feel included rather than chastised. Yet, that is not freedom and love; it is bondage. And when we step outside of the boxes and expectations of what "should be," we experience shame and condemnation.

Typically, our motivation connected to a group or people system is either to gain rewards for the earthly self or avoid some form of punishment. As such, we lose contact with the present moment because we are more focused on the future rewards or potential consequences of our behaviors. We seek earthly treasures from earthly "authorities" rather than heavenly treasures from the True Authority that loves with a true love. We cannot serve two masters, for we will love the one and despise the other. And yet, the power of systems is an authority that is blinding. It is a force that powerfully draws our attention to it rather than to the unfailing love of Christ. Systems are, in one way, anti-Christ authority because they blind and seduce us into bowing to the rules, authority, and leaven of the Pharisees again in a way that takes our eyes off of the authority of Christ alone.

When a body of believers actually begins to walk in the present with a one-with kind of love, Christ alone will be the head and will move the body without earthly authorities. There will be no "leader" – for One is our Leader (Matt. 23:10); that is, Christ as the head. Any "positions" within a body, like elders for instance, will not be seeable earthly, elevated positions but unseen spiritual positions with true spiritual grace that is more about girding up and freeing others than about making decisions connected to them. Those that are part of this kind of body will not feel the eye of judgment and separateness upon them but rather the eye of Love, freedom, and peace that allows the Spirit to convict and move them in His time. Rather than experiencing pressure to conform or perform, the true body of believers, because of being present, will recognize the Lord's works and timing and, as such, participate with Him in it. "Do not arouse or awaken my love until she pleases" (Song 8:4).

Systems and control, which come from human energy, are oriented toward the material form (idols) of the earth rather than the formless Spirit. Any energy that moves us or any source that causes us to take action – that is not God Himself – hinders our hearing and learning from God. That energy and authority serves that which is earthly and its parent, the devil. Energy that comes from the Spirit alone, however, serves the formless and unseen as well as that realm's authority or Parent, the Lord. The unseen on this earth that God values and wants us to serve and love most, however, is the true self within the people we see. He seeks the unseen pearls hidden beneath the bodies of flesh and desires that they become found and freed. And He desires that we, moved by the Spirit, serve and love others such that those beautiful pearls become uncovered and shine as they were meant to shine. "For God, who said, 'Light shall shine out of darkness,' is the One who has shone in our hearts to give the light of the knowledge of the glory of God in the face of Christ" (2 Cor. 4:6).

While we, like Jesus, are not to fight against systems and the people who run them, we can be in those systems but not of them. This is just as Jesus said about being in the world but not of it. That means that we are not to do as the Pharisees did. We are not to be moved because of the rules and rewards of the systems and their leaders. We are not to define ourselves by the world of form and what is seen. When the goals and respective rewards dictated to us by the system are what motivate us, we have little choice but to become future oriented. We lose contact with the present and with the Lord's presence. We lose contact with our true identity within and have joined more with all that is seeable. But Jesus said (Jn. 5:34), "Not that I accept human testimony," as well as (Jn. 5:41), "I do not accept praise from men." He demonstrated the importance of not attaching to earthly identity and what people's earthly, old self would say or believe about Him. Not trusting the worldly systems or the separating flesh of man was crucial to Jesus walking in a way that the ruler of the world "had nothing in Him."

Attachment to earthly identity and its power to cause lack of faith is seen in Jesus' hometown people who could not accept or know Him apart from His previous earthly roles. Jesus' hometown people said about Him (Mk. 6:3), "'Isn't this the carpenter? Isn't this Mary's son and the brother of James, Joseph, and Judas and Simon? Aren't His sisters here with us?' And *they took offense at Him*." Isn't this clear how focused and bound the people were regarding Jesus' earthly identity? Then it states that Jesus was "amazed at their lack of faith" (Mk. 6:6). This word "amazed" is also translated as "marveled" or "wondered" and is only used one other time in the scriptures about Jesus' view of others. Here Jesus uses it in the direction of *unbelief – rooted in people's strong earthly identity and roles.* The other place Jesus used the expression of wonder or amazement was regarding the centurion who said that he knew that Jesus was one with authority like himself. But Jesus' wonder in this statement is about the centurion's *belief in the unseen realm.* The centurion knew that Jesus had unseen servants that would do His bidding without question. In other words, the centurion's faith allowed him to leave behind earthly identity and form and to trust the true unseen realm and identity of Jesus. These two opposite poles regarding Jesus' amazement have to do with faith in the unseen identity and realm versus lack of faith. But as seen in these examples, Jesus saw faith in the unseen realm and identity as unusual and striking, just as He was also struck by people's extreme lack of faith distinctly because of the restrictiveness of earthly identity, roles, and form as a whole.

When we are not alert to the seduction of the world of form – of the system, its rules and rewards, the status and identity connected to the system, and the old self that gains identity from systems – we succumb to the leaven of the Pharisees. We become hooked by the world of form and all the pain that it creates because of its goal of separateness that brings aloneness and corruption. In fact, the system rewards separateness and self-glory; and when we are moved by the system and its rewards, the ego, or old self, within us is always strengthened.

We can see more about the leaven of the Pharisees and the world's rewards through the story of the rich young ruler. When Jesus said how impossible it was for rich men to enter the kingdom of heaven, it contradicted the teaching of the Pharisees that God favored those who were rich. That's why the disciples asked Jesus in astonishment, "Then who can be saved?" The leaven or teaching was such that no one could be saved if the rich weren't going to be saved. And yet, the rich young ruler believed he kept all the commandments, was rich, and still felt a sense of lack. While it is commonly recognized that he wouldn't have been perfect in obeying the commandments, his lack was still centered in something more that Jesus addressed very squarely. Jesus said (Matt. 19:21), "If you want to be perfect [complete], go, sell your possessions and give to the poor, and you will have treasure in heaven. Then come, follow Me." Through selling what he had, giving it to the poor, and following Jesus, this man would not have been able to remain in his separate, earthly identity. He would have come to learn that by losing the old self and its separate identity he was not separate but one with Jesus and with all. That's why immediately following this situation, Jesus told his disciples that it was easier for a camel to go through the eye of a needle than for a rich man (with the earthly self and life working well) to enter the kingdom of heaven. An earthly rich man typically builds up more and more distinction and separateness from others. It is the separate old self building its own, distinct identity and earthly kingdom that causes emptiness and aloneness (and the experience of lack as a whole).

Just following the interaction with the rich young ruler, Jesus stated to His disciples (Matt. 19:29), "And everyone who has left houses or brothers or sisters or father or mother or children or fields for My sake will receive a hundred times as much and will inherit eternal life." Jesus' emphasis here was for us to leave our separateness. That is, if we want to enter the way of true life, even here on this earth, it means no longer clinging to things or people as a form of separate identity from others. When those earthly things and people are our identity, we have not left them in a sense. Defining ourselves by form only causes separateness from others. It is an earthly identity, which is all tied into the old self and its ways of separation for some kind of self-glory. Defining yourself by your family, job, gifts or abilities, gender, culture, or race all serve to make distinctions and separateness in some way from others. To define yourself as rich and intelligent requires that there are those who are poor and stupid. It is all about the ego, the old self that separates for some kind of earthly distinction and glory. Earthly identities and roles as definitions of self restrict true love and true identity. When we leave earthly identities and roles as definitions of self, however, we find true life abundantly.

Jesus' parable that immediately followed all of His above discussion connected to the rich young ruler was the parable of the workers in the vineyard. In the end of that parable, the landowner asked the foreman to pay the same wages to all the workers, those that worked all day and those that worked varying portions of the day. Even though all workers were paid what had been agreed upon, those that worked the whole day grumbled saying (Matt. 20:12), "*You have made them equal to us* who have borne the burden of the work and the heat of the day." Can you hear in this grumbling how we work earthly-wise to become distinct and separate? That is the old self that wants to be separate, and yet Jesus' emphasis is on us having no earthly separation or distinction. That is why Paul exhorted the Corinthians about separating from one another. Paul stated (1 Cor 1:11-13), "For I have been informed concerning you, my brethren, by Chloe's people, that there are quarrels among you. Now I mean this, that each one of you is saying, 'I am of Paul,' and 'I of Apollos,' and 'I of Cephas,' and 'I of Christ.' Has Christ been divided?" Paul saw the old self's propensity toward separation through the labels we put upon ourselves and others (like all the denominations and various religions today). Labeling divides Christ. Do you hear that Paul even uses "I am of Christ" as an example of a way that we can separate from others? There is no love in separation. While there is nothing wrong in calling oneself a Christian, is it used in a separating kind of way? If it is, even that is of the old self, and it divides and essentially tears down rather than loves. The Pharisees' propensity toward separateness between people is exactly what they were so upset about when Jesus sat with the prostitutes and tax gatherers. Jesus' position toward not separating from one another is also what the Pharisees despised when He indicated that they (the Pharisees) were not to be "seated in the chair of Moses" (Matt. 23:2) – for they saw themselves with elevated, earthly authority and as mediators between God and man like Moses had been. The Pharisees wanted places of honor and to be separate and distinct. That is all the old self that is of the earth in its pursuit of a separate, glorious earthly identity.

In contrast to the earthly identity, however, the scriptures say (Gal. 3:26-28), "You are all sons of God through faith in Christ Jesus, for all of you who were baptized into Christ have clothed yourselves with Christ. There is neither Jew nor Greek, slave nor free, male nor female, for you are all one in Christ Jesus." There is no separation. Here again we can see the emphasis on not having separate identities according to the earth. That energy toward separation is the old self with its earthly attachments again. It is the leaven of the worldly systems. And as sons and daughters who have clothed ourselves in Christ, we are to walk in a way that does not bow to separation, just as Jesus walked loving all who would receive His love. We are to love all as if we are actually loving Him. When we've done it to the least of these, we have done it to Jesus. Why? The mystery of Christ is within all people (Col. 1:27), and the Lord desires to complete all in Christ for whoever is willing. When we injure or help another person, we have done it to Christ, for He is within all (whether or not a person acknowledges or honors He who is within).

When Jesus was asked about which commandment was the greatest, how did He answer? Take a moment to consider how He answered before you read further.

Most everyone that answers this question begins immediately with what Jesus quoted from the Old Testament: "Love the Lord your God with all your heart" and so on. And most everyone recognizes what Jesus said next as well about "loving your neighbor as yourself" as the second greatest commandment. However, when asked this question, virtually no one remembers that, in the Gospel of Mark, Jesus added a significant statement to the beginning of this greatest commandment. Here is the fullness of what Jesus stated as the greatest commandment (Mk. 12:29), "Hear, O Israel, the Lord *our* God, *the Lord is one.* Love the Lord your God with all your heart and with all your soul and with all your mind and with all your strength." Here, Jesus addresses all the people around Him, some of whom were very much against Him and His ways. And He said to all of Israel, "*Our* God, the Lord is one." In other words, our ability to follow the greatest commandment seems to depend upon the first part of what Jesus added, knowing that the Lord is "our" God and "one" God. Loving the Lord with all our heart while we are on this earth has much to do with seeing and knowing Him as one Lord over all and in all. Whereas the other peoples historically up until and during the time of Jesus worshipped many gods, separate gods over many separate things of the earth, Jesus made clear to Israel that there is one God over all – whether they believed that or not. In our minds, the Lord is not to be divided up into pieces as if He is God over certain things or certain peoples. There is not to be a separate god of the waters and seas, a god of the land, a god of provisions, or even a separate god of the Jews. Jesus meant that the Lord is God over absolutely everything and everyone, whether people label or see themselves that way or not. There is essentially one body on this earth.

Jesus' words and His greatest commandment are still to be true for us. We are to know that our Lord is the same Lord that is over all things and peoples today. The Lord is over those with different gifts than us, those in different denominations than us, those that believe completely differently than us, and yes, even over those who do not believe. The Lord will work just as He desires through believer and unbeliever alike, just like He did in Jesus' days on this earth (like He moved in Caesar Augustus to take a census that would bring Joseph and Mary to Bethlehem). While the Lord will work more fully (because of free will) within people who honor Him and desire to walk in relationship with Him, He still moves and works at times in those who do not honor or know Him. "For from Him and through Him and to Him are all things" (Rom. 11:36). Likewise, "And there are varieties of effects, but the same God who works all things in all persons" (1 Cor. 12:6). And similarly, "There is one body and one Spirit, just as also you were called in one hope of your calling; one Lord, one faith, one baptism, one God and Father of all who is over all and through all and in all" (Eph. 4:4-6).

The people of this earth have separated His body and treated Him as if He is not "one Lord." Yet, there is truly only one body of people on this earth, with the Lord God over all and in all, whether we think or label ourselves that way or not. While some people may walk as true sons and daughters (clothed) and some may not, we are nevertheless to be one people under God. God is over all and in all. That is why Jesus said the second commandment was like the first, that of loving our neighbors as ourselves. Through this commandment, Jesus squarely addressed the separateness devised by the old self when He pointed to our neighbor as being everyone, including those we have hated, despised, or seen as different from us. For when Jesus was asked who our neighbor was, He used a parable with a Samaritan representing their neighbor, and at the time, the Jews did not deal whatsoever with the Samaritans. Jesus made clear that the Lord God is one and is over all and in all people, and that we are to love Him (who is in all people) with all our heart rather than falling for the separating, unloving ways of the world and its systems. Many believers have been taught about a much smaller Christ than He truly is. Christ is truly in all and over all.

The best protection from the seduction and corruption of the world and its systems is to keep watch, not of the systems and people leading the systems, but of the old self and mind within yourself. When you keep watch of the mind of the old self and its thoughts, you will notice its temptation to draw you into joining it in gaining identity and glory somehow through the system and its people. When you see the schemes of the mind by watching with the eye of Spirit, you won't fall for or be moved by its leaven or trickery. "But you, brethren, are not in darkness, that the day should overtake you like a thief; for you are all sons of light and sons of day. We are not of night nor of darkness; so then *let us not sleep* as others do, but let us be alert and sober" (1 Thess. 5:4-7).

*Cease striving to gain identity through earthly rules, roles, and systems, which is bondage. Rather, let our identity be one-with the Lord who is one Lord and Lord of ALL.*

# BEING PRESENT AS LITTLE CHILDREN: PUTTING ON CHRIST

The Lord's final words to us through John in the book of 1 John are "Little children, guard yourselves from idols." Anything that becomes important to the extent that we are blinded and cannot see or know the Lord in it is an idol. When being present becomes so important that we strive for it, it has become an idol. During more significant difficulties, we usually question God's sovereignty or goodness, and we (really our body pain and the thinking of the old self) believe something is "wrong" at those times. That is inner resistance to what is. That is unbelief; it is distrust. And as soon as we enter a place of distrust, we participate more significantly with the flesh and we resort to "taking" again. That kind of striving to be present is an idol and is simply the old self. If you have mental anguish, pain, or anxiousness at the moment and that energy is what causes you to try to regain presence, you will not find presence. It is more important at those times to ask the Lord to help you to let go and simply wait until the energy begins to subside. As the energy lessens and is no longer the one controlling you, then you can begin to watch the old self in union with the Spirit.

Becoming truly present is never through a striving or taking. Rather, being present is always through a childlike letting go and yieldedness at the moment. Becoming present is much about stopping or no longer joining with the earthly energy of the old self that strives for something due to distrust; it is more about "Cease striving and know that I am God." We are to let go and be like little children. We simply have been so brainwashed by the way of the world and its demand for us to strive like "competent" adults that we don't see that most of what we do in life is still about striving. It is sin. That's one of the main ways of the old self that dominates us that we can't see – primarily because it is so familiar and what most of the world around us has conveyed to us throughout life.

When I am in difficult places or periods in my life, I know the main "task for me to do" is to let go. Stop. Cease striving and know that God is God – so that I don't "take" from a place of distrust. He is the God of the gospel who reaches out and saves us when we simply stop all the earthly energy and wait on Him. That is losing our life (and the old self) through the way of the cross at those times, as well as letting the Lord do the saving. Jesus said (Jn. 11:11), "Our friend Lazarus has fallen asleep; but I go, that *I may awaken him* out of sleep." Lazarus is a "type" of the church that has been asleep and not present, conscious, or awake, but the Lord is presently awakening us and causing us to be present in the light of His presence. Some who have ears to hear have been practicing the discipline of watching and being present in the light of His presence for a while. Others are gradually coming to be awakened as the Lord continues working this deeper way of the cross into His people, a sacrificial way that trusts Him enough to be present with each moment. As Jesus said during a storm, "Do not be afraid; it is I." So, let us not be afraid. It is He, the God of the gospel reaching out, who awakens and saves us – when we let Him.

The more God's people become awakened and walk more fully trusting Him with each present moment, the more we will begin to see the mysteries of Christ unfold. We will see the heavens being opened. Just like Jacob saw as a gate of heaven, where angels were ascending and descending on a ladder connecting earth to heaven, we will begin to see as well when walking more in the simplicity of the present. Jesus stated this very similar statement (about the angels ascending and descending on a ladder) to Nathanael who was under the fig tree. Along with that statement, the scriptures make a point, seemingly out of the blue, about Jesus exclaiming that Nathanael was a man with no guile. I have read that verse many times previously while wondering what that unusual point was all about. In the gospel of John it is written (1:47-51), "Jesus saw Nathanael coming to Him, and said of him, 'Behold, an Israelite indeed, *in whom is no guile!'* … And He said to him, 'Truly, truly, I say to you, you shall see the heavens opened, and the angels of God ascending and descending on the Son of Man.'" The Son of Man is the ladder who connects earth and heaven when we walk His way of the cross. Walking the way of the cross is a simple walk that trusts God's sovereignty in the present moment such that one loses the old self and its guile. Guile is rooted in deceitfulness, duplicity, and maneuvering for self gain. It was no coincidence that Jesus said that Nathanael who He described as having "no guile" would see the heavens opened. Having no guile and seeing the heavens opened go together. Only those who are childlike and walk in the simple present moment without the double-minded guile of the old self maneuvering for self-gain will see the heavens opened. Let us ask to be without the guile of the old self like Nathanael.

We are to stop seeking in a way that is striving. We are to cease striving, even spiritually. When Jesus said to seek with all our heart, soul, and mind, He meant an inward opening up to God's provisions that already and always are. We are to seek the kingdom that is "at hand," which is by opening up to it from within, for Jesus said the kingdom was within us. When God banished Adam and Eve from the garden of Eden, He merely banished them from a way of life that had everything materially the way they wanted it. Even when they were in the garden of Eden, they still were dissatisfied with what was. That is still the root of our sin. We do not trust God when life is not the way we want it. But we are still in the garden. It is the world; it has just changed form. We are still with God. We still have available at every moment what is sovereignly right and good for us. He and His kingdom are still at hand, but we still treat Him like we want and need something different than what He provides in each present moment.

Being discontent with God's provisions in the present is what we are to repent of. Repent means to change the way we are walking. We are to walk being content with God's provisions, with "what is" rather than to want something different or more. As we accept God's provisions regarding what is, then we find more and abundant life – because He always is. When we seek the kingdom that is at hand, we find there is life unending. The scriptures say (Ps. 17:15), "As for me, I shall behold Thy face in righteousness; I will be *satisfied with Thy likeness when I awake.*" When we are present and awake, we will find that we are content and satisfied. When we accept God's provisions as is, we learn, grow, and become transformed more into the full being we were meant to be that is in His image. Really, this "growing" is about receiving more of the fullness of His likeness regarding what has already been given and is planted inside us. We just finally come into union with and possess what had been given.

In contrast, we are unable to learn or grow when we are discontent with God's provisions and the moment as it is. When we are not content with His kingdom that is at hand, we fail to receive of it; we fail to enter into it. *Redemption comes through contentment, whereas destruction comes through discontentment.* Let us be as little children that can play as easily with a cardboard box as with a shiny bought toy.

When we are discontent about life, others, or even self in some way, the old self is governing us. Being discontent is always under a false lens and causes a maneuvering or "buying and selling" for gain in life. When Jesus took a scourge, entered the temple, and drove out all who were buying and selling there (Matt. 21:12-16; Jn. 2:13-22), that is a picture of what He does with "our temple and its fleshly garment, the old self, who buys and sells." Just like in the book of Revelation (13:16-18), only those who have the mark or number of the beast can "buy and sell," which is 666, the number of man. The number of man (and of the beast) has to do with the old self who is always about selfish gain. That old self is what Jesus essentially keeps driving out of us through the scourgings from life in various ways – *so that we become freed* to walk in our true identities that are free from the world and its destructiveness. When Jesus drove out those who were buying and selling in the temple, He said (Matt. 21:13), "My house will be called a house of prayer, but you are making it a den of robbers." When we walk in our true identity, we are automatically a house of prayer and worship that serves God. When we walk in the old self and identity, however, we are automatically a den of robbers or thieves that buy and sell for gain. And when the chief priests and teachers of the law heard the children crying out, "Hosanna to the Son of David," they became indignant. Jesus then questioned them about not having heard, "From the lips of children and infants you have ordained praise." Here again, this whole exchange is symbolic of our own walks with the Lord. When we walk in our true identities, we are children and infants, not of men, but of the Lord Himself who cry out in praise giving witness to Him. And when we are the true children we were meant to be, we will encounter people of the worldly systems becoming indignant with us.

Immediately after Jesus drove out from the temple those who were buying and selling, He cursed a fig tree when He found no fruit on it to eat (Matt. 21:18-22). This, once more like Jesus scourging the old self who buys and sells so as to free us, is about Him cursing the old self that has no true fruit. He curses the old self so that it cannot produce good fruit. That is the only way for us to let go of the old self and become the true identity and child we were meant to be. The old self becoming cursed and poor is the only way for us to let go of it such that we finally embrace the truth of the new wine that is better than the old wine. The old has to taste bad for us to stop drinking of it. Jesus wants us freed from the old self that is always discontent and working toward gain by buying and selling in some way. We have simply clung to the old self and its identity because of not believing that there is so much more abundant life that is beyond it – not through striving for something different or better, but through embracing the identity within that God has already provided.

When our old self, along with its systems and schemes, is stripped from us by the way of the cross in our lives, love remains. All else falls away, and love, that which is of God and His likeness, remains. God's works and love do not occur through our strivings but through His reigning in our lives when the old self no longer dominates. Like in the parable of the sower, the bad soil of the old self is the ground that has no richness or depth and only produces thorns and thistles because of the worries and difficulties of the world. It produces no true fruit because *it does not allow the word to grow.* However, the good ground (Mk. 4:20) is our true identity that neither strives nor worries *because we accept God's word of life that comes upon us, difficulties and all.* That is truly good ground. He, then, produces fruit, thirty, sixty, and hundred-fold through that vessel. For clarification, however, accepting God's word of life is not passivity regarding life (as was mentioned earlier). Rather, accepting God's word is first accepting and honoring "what is" so that there is freedom from within us for God to be able to move us how He knows is best. That may be to continue accepting the situation, addressing it in some way, or leaving it (temporarily or permanently). But it is always about us first accepting a situation for God to have the freedom to work in and through us with His more abundant life as opposed to our limited earthly reactions and ways that produce no heavenly fruit.

Redemption and its fruits occur when we become one-with the totality of God's word of life. The Lord is bigger than and in all that we encounter, and when life is oriented in or flows a certain direction, that is the Lord and His oneness in all things. He is the glue that holds all things together and works all things together for good, and we can either accept or resist His word of life. When we are discontent and resist Him, His Provisions, and Life, we step in the old self and His fruits are choked out by us (really, by the old self). In contrast, when we are content with and accept Him and His Provisions through Life, redemption and His fruits take place in us and through us to this world. When we want nothing different from Life and become one-with the totality of how He presently works in life, His totality and fullness (rather than our energy and effort) perform works through us that transform us and those around us for further expressing Him.

Jesus said (Mk. 4:26-29), "This is what the kingdom of God is like. A man scatters seed on the ground. Night and day, whether he sleeps or gets up, the seed sprouts and grows, though he does not know how. *All by itself the soil produces grain* — first the stalk, then the head, then the full kernel in the head. As soon as the grain is ripe, he puts the sickle to it, because the harvest has come." We so often try too hard to get the things of God to grow. But Jesus said the kingdom is not like that. *The good soil alone produces the growth without effort* – when our old self is simply out of the way such that our true identity within has freedom to be. That good soil is when we are simply like a child in our true identity rather than in the old self, which is the "competent" adult that attempts to maneuver and control life because of not trusting love. **True Love and identity simply burst forth not by striving and effort but by fasting, resting from, and discontinuing participation with the dominance of the old self. Cease striving so that you have the room to truly experience that God is God.**

We as a people have yet to discover how much our earthly energy is constantly busy and moving such that we interfere with experiencing God as God. One energy must decrease so the other, the true, can increase. Simply being still more regularly automatically provides room for God and His energy to move on our behalf so as to make Himself known. The good ground simply produces growth when it is given a chance, which occurs by us not participating with the old ground.

The true identity is the good ground and the old self is the bad. When we accept Life as it is and surrender to its Way, He and our true identity with Him will come forth and reign. It's the good soil that produces the growth, nothing else – because the good soil is of God. On the cross, Jesus said, "It is finished." The work was forever finished and will keep flourishing when we simply trust that He and His presence will go forth when the cross of life reduces the old self. Jesus said that the lilies and grass are beautifully clothed and then stated (Matt. 6:30), "Will God not much more clothe you?" Can you hear in that verse how we become clothed? The Lord automatically clothes us without our effort. Yet, He does not violate free will when we function from the old self that tries to clothe ourselves throughout life. Most times, He is simply interested in a ceasing of the old so that we become like children and allow Him to move freely in and through our lives. Then He automatically becomes the resurrection life in and through us.

A simple test has helped me to recognize when either the old self or true identity is governing me at the moment. When I truly desire to be present with Christ at the moment and am able to simply be, there is always peace. When there is not peace in the present moment, it automatically means I am striving for or pursuing something more than Him alone. An idol beyond being with Him at the moment exists, whether it is expectations of myself, others, or life. But generally, it comes down to the choice of "being with Jesus" or "pursuing something more or other than Jesus." It is like being in one filing cabinet or the other. One provides contentment and peace, and the other, discontentment and lack of peace.

Being content versus discontent is critical to remaining present in our walk, as well as for remaining in our true identity. Paul learned a great secret. That is, he learned to be content in all things. When we experience discontentment or a supposed "gap" of any kind regarding where we think we or life "should" be, that is always the old self with its lies. Body pain always and only sees a gap regarding what ought to be. However, as Paul said, "Our adequacy is in Christ." We've heard those words many times before but, often times, they've only been words to us. It is a fact.

There is never really any gap. You might think, "Of course there is." Yes, of course there always is in the old self. And if that's who you believe you are at any given moment in life, there will always be gaps. But if you believe you are the "new creation," an identity that has been made in Christ (as opposed to your various earthly identities), there is never any gap. You cannot find true rest and peace unless you abide in your true identity in Him that has no gaps. You cannot rest in joy and love unless you know yourself as the new name that is one-spirit with Him that has no lack.

Christ is always the gap filler. That's why the Lord said to Paul, "My grace is sufficient for you." While Paul likely experienced and perceived a gap at that point in his walk, Christ essentially made clear to him that there was no gap. His grace fills in all the gaps and it is enough as it is – until, if He so chooses, gives the grace or "ability" to walk differently than we currently do. But the truth of the matter is, our true identity within is already perfected and spotless. Most people simply have rarely abided in that true identity and place that needs nothing else. And abiding there means believing that that identity is us. The miraculous part of all of this is, that when we abide there and view that as our home and identity, we become free from the rules, expectations, and demands of the old self and the world for which it lives. Do you see that when we abide within the mystery of Christ placed within us as our identity, the world has no ground in us and cannot touch us in a destructive way? We walk more as Christ actually walked because we are grounded in Him, but the key is to abide in and know ourselves as that true identity that is already perfected in Him. Only when we leave that true identity in our minds and instead join with the old self do we become vulnerable to walking in the world's sins again.

When we finally come to a place of really believing our identity is truly in Christ, that place does not need furthered, perfected, or changed in any way. That is who we were created to be; it was a gift that we were to possess by our souls simply being in agreement with the Lord. Our adequacy is in Christ, not anything having to do with the old self that always experiences gaps. We just haven't possessed this identity yet because we haven't believed the Lord's words as actually true. Just like in the garden of Eden, Adam and Eve were able to be convinced that something more was needed. For us, even after recognizing that we are to have our adequacy in Christ, and that the cross already finished any work needed, we still believe the lie of the old self that something more is needed. We still think there are actually gaps when our old self has walked in sin. Believing that lie of something more being needed is the very thing that keeps us from walking in the freedom, love, and power that were meant to come with our new, already perfected identity.

When we believe that we are already the new identity and simply are to join with Christ in that identity, and that there is no gap, we are free from that old identity with all of its rules and demands from the world. None of those worldly things truly apply to us when we know who we truly are. When I say that they don't apply to us, I mean regarding identity. While we are still under the world's systems, rules, and government, we are not of it. We submit to the rules but we no longer define ourselves at all by them. They are meaningless to who we truly are. Can you sense the freedom in this? *Much of the pain that we've walked under in life is tied to believing we still are the old self who only has the option of defining itself by the world and its expectations.* We become sad, discouraged, fearful, and hopeless all because of falsely perceiving ourselves as having some kind of lack because of defining ourselves by the world's standards. As we begin to see, however, that we are truly a new creation in Christ that has no gaps – no further place we should be but are already adequate and perfected right where we are – we actually begin to walk more like Jesus walked. We are freed to walk in love and His goodness rather than in shame and condemnation according to the world. But this kind of walk only comes from truly knowing who we are in Him. Sufficiency already exists – just like in the garden of Eden and just like was the case for Paul. It is only a lie when we perceive some kind of gap about where we should be that is "further or better" than where we currently are. The lens is completely of the old self when we don't know that we are already sufficient and adequate in Him as we are. Do you hear that believing we are truly the sufficient identity within is *how* much of the power comes for walking the way that Christ walked?

When we have walked in places of sin or apparent lack at a given point, it is as Paul said (Rom. 7:20), "It is no longer *I* who do it, but it is sin living in me that does it." In other words, Paul's "I" was him standing in his new creation or identity in Christ. We can hear very clearly that Paul saw himself as the "I" who cannot or does not sin. He saw a perfect and pure "I." When Paul said "I," he saw one who was one-spirit with Christ, and that the other part, the old self, who still sinned had *nothing* to do with who he really was. Sin was dead to him and didn't count in a way that defined him whatsoever. That is a clear picture of standing in his true identity, an identity that freed him from the weight of the world and its power to define, control, and psychologically defeat him. There was no inadequacy. Nothing needed added to this true identity, even when the old self sinned. In Paul's mind, the mind controlled by the Spirit rather than the flesh, he was already perfect and sufficient in Christ with no gaps needing to be filled. Paul was an example for us about embracing our true identity. He didn't shrink back from already seeing himself as the unseen new name and identity even though the Lord was still redeeming his walk. In fact, Paul's embracing of his new self and pure, true identity was likely how he was so powerfully redeemed and restored. That was also likely how he was used as a trusting, childlike vessel for the Lord's purposes.

Our new identity is crucial for a powerfully redeeming walk such that we know love and are a vessel of love for others. The scriptures exhort us many times in various ways to put on this new identity in Him. We are to clothe ourselves or "put on" fine linens, white garments, the armor of light, the full armor of God, the imperishable, love, and the new self as seen below:

- Let us therefore lay aside the deeds of darkness and *put on the armor of light* (Rom. 13:12).

- But you did not learn Christ in this way, if indeed you have heard Him and have been taught in Him, just as truth is in Jesus, that, in reference to your former manner of life, you lay aside the old self, which is being corrupted in accordance with the lusts of deceit, and that you be renewed in the spirit of your mind, and *put on the new self,* which in the likeness of God has been *created in righteousness and holiness of the truth* (Eph. 4:20-24).

- Finally, be strong in the Lord, and in the strength of His might. *Put on the full armor of God,* that you may be able to stand firm against the schemes of the devil (Eph. 6:10-11).

- And beyond all these things *put on love,* which is the perfect bond of unity (Col. 3:14).

- I advise you to buy from Me gold refined by fire, that you may become rich, and *white garments, that you may clothe yourself,* and that the shame of your nakedness may not be revealed (Rev. 3:18).

- And the armies which are in heaven, *clothed in fine linen, white and clean,* were following Him on white horses… And on His robe and on His thigh He has a name written, "KING OF KINGS, AND LORD OF LORDS" (Rev. 19:14-16).

- And one of the elders answered, saying to me, "These who are *clothed in the white robes,* who are they, and from where have they come?" (Rev. 7:13).

- *He who overcomes shall thus be clothed in white garments* (Rev. 3:5).

- For this perishable must *put on the imperishable,* and

this mortal must *put on immortality*. But when this perishable will have put on the imperishable, and this mortal will have put on immortality, then will come about the saying that is written, "Death is swallowed up in victory. O death, where is your victory? O death, where is your sting?" (1 Cor. 15:53-55).

Another verse is similar to all of the above (Rom. 13:14): "But *put on the Lord Jesus Christ*, and make no provision for the flesh in regard to its lusts." Which is it? Put on Christ or put on and clothe ourselves with all of the other things mentioned above? It is both; it is one and the same. To put on the new self or any of the other qualities has to do with putting on the imperishable Christ. That is why He leads an army and is called "King of Kings." Christ is called that because we essentially become kings who are one-with Him, the true King who leads us. When we take on our true identity, as Paul did, it is the perfect Christ within that we take on as us. The portion of Christ within becomes us as we abide in Him and that identity. That is why the scriptures state that "death is swallowed up in victory." Death can no longer touch us because we no longer define ourselves by the earthly roles and identities. Death doesn't sting or even pertain to us when we know who we truly are, the unseen portion of Christ within. We are not the old self who does have shortcomings, but rather, we are the imperishable identity in Christ that needs nothing added.

*"Awake, awake,* clothe yourself in your strength, O Zion; clothe yourself in your beautiful garments, O Jerusalem, the holy city. *For the uncircumcised and the unclean will no more come into you* [when we remain in that true identity]. Shake yourself from the dust, rise up, O captive Jerusalem; loose yourself from the chains around your neck, O captive daughter of Zion" (Isa. 52:1-2). Let us clothe ourselves in our true identity, which already is one-with the presence of the Lord. Let it be as the scriptures have said (Num. 32:32), "We ourselves will cross over *armed in the presence of the Lord* into the land of Canaan."

Lord, help us to believe. Help us join with and walk in the fullness of our new identity that is already perfected, spotless, righteous, and holy in You. Help us to recognize that walking and abiding in You in this way is the power of redemption and restoration into all true goodness even while walking in this world. Help us to be like children who simply trust in this miraculous identity and goodness that You've placed as a treasure within us. Help us to sell all else that we would desire this one pearl of wisdom within that is not of this world. Help us to overcome – to cease the striving of the old self and identity so as to be freed into the true. And thank You for giving of Yourself that we might know and abide in You, Your love, and Your riches that are beyond the limits of this world. Amen.

*Be still; dwell often on your true identity in Him who is perfect and needs nothing added, as opposed to staring at the inadequacy of the old self. Yet, as a child, simply ask Him to help you regularly abide in and know your true self as one-with True Security Within that is not attached to anything earthly.*

# Songs of Identity and Being Present

Let us end by having our hearts dwell on Christ in the way He is moving in this day about true identity and being present, for the scriptures state (Col 3:16): "Let the word of Christ richly dwell within you, with all wisdom teaching and admonishing one another with psalms and hymns and spiritual songs, singing with thankfulness in your hearts to God." The following are four related songs that the Spirit worked within me during my journey, two of which were birthed during these writings about walking in the present in our true identity. The last two songs have to do with trusting the Lord to work and fight on our behalf to release our true identity in Him. You may want to read or sing these songs as prayers or poems, and as reminders of walking in the present in our true identity.

Song 1: <u>Help Me Be in the Now</u>

1. Being present with You, is my worship so true.
   In the present, with I AM, is the Way of the Lamb.
   For when the present I lose, it's not really You that I choose,
   So help me to be in the now, that only to You I would bow –
   That Your Presence would rise in me, Lord.
   So help me be in the now. Help me be in the now.

2. When I'm not in the now, there is old ground to plow.
   For the future and past, are just lies I must fast.
   'Cause they are only in vain, and always bring suffering and pain.
   For only the present is real, that the future and past try to steal –
   From Your Presence that can rise in me, Lord.
   So help me be in the now. Help me be in the now.

3. When I watch with Your eyes, my new self begins to rise.
   For I learn who I am, when I watch with the Lamb.
   For the old self just withers away, and one-spirit with You, I grow each day.
   So help me to walk without shame, and to shine in my glorious
      new name –
   That Your Presence would rise in me, Lord.
   So help me be in the now. Help me be in the now.

Song 2: <u>True Identity</u> (Who Was this "I" that Did Not Sin?)

1. When Paul said about a battle deep within, a battle about sin,
   There's a secret not well known, though the seed has long been sown.
   Identity, true identity.

2. When sin showed though he did not choose that course, he saw
   the darkened source.
   And he said it was not "I," but the sin that did not die.
   Identity, true identity.

   Who was this "I" with no earthly name? Who was this "I" that had no shame?
   Who was this "I" perfect and free? This kind of "I" I'm to learn
   to be?
   I am simply to be a child who is no longer hiding.
   I am simply to be God's child who is truly abiding …
   In true identity, in true identity.

3. When Paul saw that the sin was not of him, but the old self dark
   and dim,
   Then he knew that he was free, perfect and spotless as can be.
   Identity, true identity.

4. So receive of this glorious gift to us, through a simple, childlike
   trust.
   It's a gift that's who we are, from the One True Morningstar.
   Identity, true identity.

   Who was this "I" that did not sin? Who was this "I" that was perfect
   within?
   Who was this "I" free from the old? This peaceful "I" that was like pure
   gold?
   I am simply to be a child with a new song to sing,
   I am simply to be God's child, yet a king with the King …
   In true identity, in true identity.

## Song 3: <u>Walk Across the Waters</u> (Simply Let Go)

1. Lord, My spirit is willing
   To follow You wherever You go,
   But my flesh filled with weakness
   Resists everything I do not know.

   For my flesh tries to stay in control,
   Though my spirit seeks to be made whole.

   So help me surrender Lord, to walk across the waters,
   As You call out my name, to trust and to know …
   To simply let go.

2. During trials I cling so tight.
   I just hold on to all that I know,
   And my flesh fights for earthly rights.
   I am fearful of just letting go.

   But the trials are needed for,
   Making my flesh humble and poor.

   So help me surrender Lord, to walk across the waters,
   As You call out my name, to trust and to know …
   To simply let go.

3. When I learn to let go,
   The fear and the pain will no longer lead me.
   Then I'll love with Your love,
   And the falsehood and the lies will no longer deceive me.

   For this heart was created for,
   Showing Your love, holy and pure.

So help me surrender Lord, to walk across the waters,
As You call out my name, to trust and to know …
To simply let go.

Song 4: I Am the Resurrection (Do You Believe in Me?)

1. I am the resurrection, and I am the Life.
   He who believeth in Me, though he dies he will live.
   Do you believe that I am your hope?
   Do you believe that I am your healer?
   Do you believe that I am fighting for you?
   Do you believe I Am? Do you believe in Me?

2. During waves that you face, know that I'm drawing you.
   You are a child of Mine and I perfectly care for you.
   Do you believe that I am your purpose?
   Do you believe that I am your enough?
   Do you believe that I am your fullness?
   Do you believe I Am? Do you believe in Me?

3. Daily death in the flesh will bring new life in you.
   Each time I raise you with Life, the new Life will be Mine.
   Do you believe that I am your Way?
   Do you believe that I am your Truth?
   Do you believe that I am your Life?
   Do you believe I Am? Do you believe in Me?

*Cease striving, abide in Him, be present, and know that God is God.*

*Be blessed.*

Breinigsville, PA USA
07 November 2010
248818BV00002B/18/P